THE GOOD, THE BAD, AND THE UGLY
KANSAS CITY CHIEFS

THE GOOD, THE BAD, AND THE UGLY KANSAS CITY CHIEFS

HEART-POUNDING, JAW-DROPPING, AND GUT-WRENCHING MOMENTS FROM KANSAS CITY CHIEFS HISTORY

Bill Althaus

TRIUMPH
BOOKS

Library of Congress Cataloging-in-Publication Data

Althaus, Bill.
    The good, the bad, and the ugly: Kansas City Chiefs:
    heart-pounding, jaw-dropping, and gut-wrenching moments
    from Kansas City Chiefs history / Bill Althaus.
        p. cm.
    Includes bibliographical references.
    ISBN-13: 978-1-57243-928-3
    ISBN-10: 1-57243-928-9
    1. Kansas City Chiefs (Football team)—History. I. Title.

GV956.K35A48 2007
796.332'6409778411—dc22

                                                    2007018196

This book is available in quantity at special discounts for your group or organization. For further information, contact:

Triumph Books
542 South Dearborn Street
Suite 750
Chicago, Illinois 60605
(312) 939-3330
Fax (312) 663-3557

Printed in U.S.A.
ISBN: 978-1-57243-928-3
Design by Patricia Frey
All photos courtesy of AP/Wide World Photos unless otherwise indicated.

*This book is dedicated to my family—
my wife Stacy and my two sons, Zach
and Sean. You mean so very much to me.
Thanks for your support.*

CONTENTS

Foreword by Len Dawson   xi

Acknowledgments   xv

The Good   1
  Lenny the Cool   1
  The NFL's First Giant   6
  One-of-a-Kind Linebacker   9
  Just Call Him "Contact"   13
  He Kicked His Way into the Hall of Fame   16
  An Unlikely Hall of Famer   22

How It All Began   26
  In Lamar Hunt's Words   26

They Weren't So Foolish After All   34
  "The Foolish Club" and the AFL   34
  Lamar "007" Hunt and the Merger of Two Leagues   42

On the Verge of Greatness   46
  Otis Taylor   46
  Mike Garrett   48
  Chris Burford   50
  Fred Arbanas   51
  Jerry Mays   52

Jerrell Wilson   54
Emmitt Thomas   54
Ed Budde   55
E.J. Holub   56
Jim Tyrer   57
Jim Lynch   58
Johnny Robinson   59
Deron Cherry   60
Nick Lowery   62
Neil Smith   63
Priest Holmes   64

It Ain't Over 'Til It's Over   67
A Day the Defense Ruled   67
Revenge Is Sweet for Chiefs   69

Coming Through in the Clutch   73
Gambling Probe No Distraction for Super
    Bowl IV MVP Dawson   73
The Nigerian Nightmare   78
The "Will" to Succeed   81
Dante's Inferno   84
Just Call These Unlikely Friends the
    Chiefs' "Odd Couple"   85
Johnson Stars When Given the Opportunity   90
Johnson Needs No Motivation   92
Green Becomes Quiet Team Leader   94

Numbers Don't Lie   97
Marty and Carl   97
Thomas Paved the Way to Chiefs' Return to Glory   100
"It's Time to Step Down"   106
Still in Search of Elusive Goal   110

The Dream Backfield   113
Joe Cool   113
Allen Leaves Lasting Legacy   118
Allen Walks Away from the Game He Loves   120

Do the Right Thing   124
   Giving Back   124
   Gonzalez Stars On and Off the Field   127

Living a Dream   131
   Out of Africa   131
   Retirement Hasn't Slowed Down Vermeil   134

The Bad   138
   Tragedy Strikes Chiefs Twice   138
   Delaney Was a True Hero   139
   Teammates Stunned by Simmons's Death   141

DT   145
   Blood Clot Claims Thomas's Life   145
   Remembering a Friend   146
   Thomas Will Never Be Forgotten   149

What Might Have Been   152
   Playing for More than Pride   152
   Chiefs Receive a Lump of Coal this Christmas Day 157
   The Game of His Life   161

The Ugly   164
   The Hall of Shame   164
   The Quarterbacks   166
   The Jail Birds   172
   The Rest of the Worst   175

What Were They Thinking?   178
   What Went So Terribly Wrong?   178
   Warfield's "Dumb, Dumb, Dumb" Move   181

Monday Night Meltdown   184
   Thomas Apologizes for Role in Monday
      Night Meltdown   184
   Smith Watches as Chiefs Self-Destruct   187

Kicked in the Gut by Some Colts   189
   Black Sunday   189
   Not Even a Priest Could Save the Chiefs   192
   The Playoffs Are a Different Beast   194

Chiefs Trivia   200
   Retired Chiefs Jersey Numbers   200
   Chasing that Playoff Dream   201

About the Author   203

FOREWORD

The Good, the Bad, and the Ugly.

I like that title. It kind of makes me chuckle as I think about past teammates and former members of the Kansas City Chiefs and try to fit them into those specific categories. I know I played with a few ugly guys, but they were awfully good teammates. Does that put me in a bad situation?

As you read this book, I hope you take a moment to reflect on what Lamar Hunt did for Kansas City, as well as Len Dawson and countless other AFL players who might never have had the opportunity to play professional football had it not been for Hunt's wisdom, foresight, and leadership. When Mr. Hunt passed away and I was asked to speak at his memorial service, I began thinking about the many lives he had touched over the years.

I would never have lived in Kansas City had it not been for Lamar. And as I stood at the podium and looked out into the audience, I saw so many individuals who could make the same statement.

When Lamar formed the AFL, he and the other owners were simply called "the Foolish Club." No one gave this new league a chance and anyone with NFL ties ran it down any time they were given the opportunity. We were the poor stepchild, the Mickey Mouse League, the league that was made up of the players who weren't good enough to make it in the NFL.

I sat on the bench for five years in the NFL, waiting for an opportunity to play. It never came. Then I heard about this new league and got excited. All I ever wanted was a chance, and Lamar gave me that chance. He gave the same chance to George Blanda and Lance Alworth and Don Maynard. Somehow, those guys found their way into the Pro Football Hall of Fame, so I guess you can't say they weren't good enough. They just needed the opportunity.

I remember the early days of the league when we practiced in public parks, shared whirlpools with opposing teams, and hung our clothes on nails in wooden lockers. The minimum salary was $5,500 and you didn't get paid for preseason games. But I wasn't in it for the money and neither were my teammates. We loved the game and simply wanted the chance to play.

When I signed with the Dallas Texans, I was surprised at just how good the talent was. We had All-Americans like Chris Burford and E.J. Holub and the league's first superstar running back, Abner Haynes. We had a great young coach in Hank Stram, who was bound and determined to succeed in his first head coaching assignment.

But most importantly, we had an owner in Lamar Hunt who not only believed in his players and his coaching staff, he believed in this new and exciting league. We were like a fraternity. Our "captain" was a defensive lineman named Jerry Mays, who was AFL through and through. He played only one season after the AFL merged with the NFL. He said he was an AFL guy and always wanted to be known as an AFL guy.

You can't imagine the pressure we faced in the first Super Bowl, because we weren't just playing for each other and the great fans in Kansas City. We were playing for an entire league. I think that's why the loss was so devastating. We worked so hard to get back to the Super Bowl and we were the last AFL team to win the world championship when we beat the NFL's Minnesota Vikings in Super Bowl IV. We were able to give Kansas City its first championship and we reveled in the fact that an AFL team had won the last game before the two leagues merged. If you wanted to see a bunch of grown men act like little kids, you should have been in our locker room after that win.

Foreword

Throughout the early years of the Kansas City Chiefs, we had a special chemistry. We all cared about each other and most of us lived and worked in Kansas City in the off-season. We would get together after games and have big family parties.

That's one thing I really miss about those good ol' days—the camaraderie that came from being part of a team like the Chiefs. Today, football is a business—a billion-dollar business. We never imagined that the Super Bowl would become such a huge event or that the league would have its own network where you could basically tune in to a game 24 hours a day.

This book traces the team through the years with stories that might bring a smile to your face or a tear to your eye. The history of this team is rich with characters, Hall of Famers, and first-class individuals, and it all starts with Lamar. I only wish he were here so he could flip through the pages, smile in approval, and say, "Job well done."

—Len Dawson

ACKNOWLEDGMENTS

A book about the history of a team that has a rich tradition like the Kansas City Chiefs can be a bit intimidating. Many thanks go out to the steady hand and guidance I received from Bob Snodgrass. I hope you realize how much I value your guidance. To Bob Moore, Pete Moris, Patrick Herb, and Brad Kuhbander of the Chiefs public relations department, who allowed me to take over their vault of information, thus making this book possible. Thanks for all you do for me and the rest of the media in Kansas City. To Lamar Hunt, who was so excited about this project. I know that somewhere Mr. Hunt is smiling and nodding in approval. To the one and only Len Dawson, who gave so much of his time to make this project special. Len, I don't care what you say, you are a Kansas City icon and will never be forgotten.

THE GOOD

LENNY THE COOL

Sitting behind the anchor desk on the set of the KMBC-TV 6:00 news, Len Dawson still has the commanding presence that helped him become one of the most successful quarterbacks in the history of both the AFL and the NFL.

He still has a square chin, trim build, and long, perfectly manicured fingers that threw tight, perfect spirals during a 14-year career that saw him win a Super Bowl Most Valuable Player award and earn his place among the game's immortals in the Pro Football Hall of Fame.

Under his leadership, the franchise won three AFL titles and a world championship. He earned the nickname "Lenny the Cool" because no matter what situation he faced, he never blinked when facing danger.

"Lenny was just a remarkable leader and quarterback," former Chiefs coach Hank Stram said. "He was cool, but I called him the quiet assassin. He said a lot with expressions. He never had to open his mouth because he said a lot with his eyes."

When a teammate fouled up, Dawson never said a word.

"He didn't need to," said former running back Ed Podolak. "He'd just give you a quick glance and you'd know what he was thinking. We all respected Lenny. He was our leader and he was the Chiefs."

Dawson didn't just earn that respect on the playing field; he was oftentimes at his best during a demanding practice session.

"I remember one practice when it was about 105 degrees with 95 percent humidity. It was so hot you couldn't breathe. It was like practicing in a sauna. Coach Stram had a thing called the Winning Edge, which was a series of drills we did before practice even began. I mean, they knocked you out."

During one lackluster practice session, the Chiefs coach stopped practice. Sitting atop his cherry picker, a device Stram had placed on the back of a truck and carted out to the field so he could get an overview of the entire practice session, Stram demanded that his players go through the Winning Edge.

"There was a lot of moaning and groaning, and all of a sudden Lenny yells, 'He ain't gonna kill me. I love this!' And he takes off and begins doing the drills. If that's not leadership, I don't know what is."

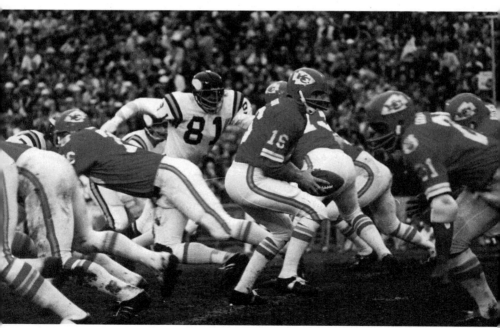

Hall of Famer Len Dawson (No. 16), shown here in Super Bowl IV against the Minnesota Vikings, was a cool customer on and off the field.

When asked about the incident, Dawson simply smiled.

"I didn't say much," Dawson said. "I didn't need to. But when I did, the guys took notice. It's a compliment that Ed would remember something like that after all these years."

Today, instead of calling the plays for the Chiefs, Dawson provides expert commentary on 101 The Fox, the Chiefs Radio Network, where he serves as an award-winning color analyst.

"I was one of the first pro athletes to take a television job," Dawson said, pausing a moment to recall how many years he'd been at Channel 9. "When we moved to Kansas City from Dallas, they talked to me about being a sports anchor. I thought it sounded interesting, so we would get done with practice at 5:30, I'd shower and get to the studio and do the 6:00 newscast. Then I'd go home, have dinner with my family, and go back and do the 10:00 show. I had someone ask me the other day if there was anyplace I like to go when I'm not working, and I told them, 'I'm always working.' I've been doing this for 40 years."

Believe it or not, his schedule is less hectic now than it once was. When he retired from the Chiefs in 1975, he worked network broadcasts for NBC and hosted *Inside the NFL* on HBO. He would leave on Tuesdays for New York, tape the HBO program on Wednesdays, and catch a flight back so he could anchor the 10:00 PM news that evening.

"I'm too old for that now," said Dawson, who looks years younger than 72. "But I still enjoy my work here at Channel 9 and I enjoy working with the Chiefs. When I left NBC, I began broadcasting Chiefs games back in 1984—during the down years. They just weren't very good back then. It was pretty lean until Carl [Peterson] and Marty [Schottenheimer] came in 1989. They turned things around and there was no more exciting place in the NFL than Arrowhead Stadium on a Sunday afternoon.

"I don't know if the fans here realize how highly regarded they are around the league and by our opponents. It's tough to play at Arrowhead because it's so noisy. That sea of red really makes a difference. Just ask our coaches or our players."

Unlike many former players who become announcers, Dawson doesn't believe in sugarcoating what's taking place out on the field.

"I just tell the listener what I see. If I see a bad play, I call it a bad play. Then I try to explain what happened. It's almost like watching game film with a player. You go through what happened and analyze it. I really think that the transition from sports to the real world was made easier because of my broadcasting career."

While many of today's Chiefs fans may think of Dawson as an announcer, he now stands alongside Kansas City Royals Hall of Famer George Brett and golfing legend Tom Watson as a Kansas City sports icon.

But it didn't begin that way for the former Purdue All-American, who sat the bench for five years with the NFL's Pittsburgh Steelers and Cleveland Browns before finally getting the chance to join his former Purdue assistant coach, Stram, who was now coaching in the new AFL.

"I asked for my release from the Browns because I had to go and see if I could still get the job done," Dawson said. "I hadn't played since Purdue and I didn't know if I could still play quarterback. I started two games and didn't finish either one of them. I played about five quarters in five years and didn't really have a lot of confidence."

Dawson saw Stram at a coaching convention in Cleveland and they later met for lunch.

"Hank asked me how things were going and I was honest with him. I told him I wasn't very happy and he said he'd love to have me with this new team he was coaching in Dallas [the Dallas Texans moved to Kansas City in 1963]. Hank was going to an All-Star game in Buffalo, so he stopped in Pittsburgh and I went to the airport to meet him. I signed the contract and was ready for a new opportunity with a great coach and a new league."

When Dawson arrived in Dallas, Stram didn't really know what to expect.

"Lenny wasn't very good when he first came down to Dallas," Stram said. "A friend of mine watched one practice and he said, 'That quarterback is going to get you fired.'"

Dawson knew he needed to shake off the rust, but he didn't realize just how rusty his entire game had become while languishing on the bench with two NFL teams.

"I was just plain terrible. My timing was off, I didn't have any footwork, anything I had done at Purdue had just about disappeared. But Hank stuck with me; he had more faith in me than I had in myself. He would break down my game—the stance, ball handling, footwork, your release, everything. Hank was so patient, and I will always be grateful to him and Lamar [Hunt, the team owner]. If it hadn't been for Hank, I'd have been out of pro football and if it hadn't been for Mr. Hunt moving the team to Kansas City, well, I don't know what path my life might have taken. When we heard we were moving to Kansas City we all thought it was some cow town. We didn't know anything about it. Now, just think of all the players over the years who still live here. It's pretty remarkable."

It's not quite as remarkable as the transformation Dawson made under Stram's tutelage.

"I finally felt like I'd put it all together by the final preseason game. Things were coming back to me. I started the opener against Boston and played well and all of a sudden football was fun again."

Dawson and the Dallas Texans won the AFL championship in the third year of the new league. When they moved to Kansas City, they became the toast of the Midwest.

"Well, that took a while," Dawson said, chuckling. "There were a lot of empty seats those first two years in Kansas City. But Hank built a great offensive and defensive team. We had Jan [Stenerud], one of the best kickers in the history of the game, and Jerrel Wilson, a punter who should be in the Hall of Fame. We played in the first Super Bowl and lost [35–10 to the Green Bay Packers] but made it back to Super Bowl IV and won it all [23–7]."

Fellow Hall of Famer Buck Buchanan recalled back then how Dawson handled himself before that classic victory over the heavily favored Vikings.

"I'll never forget the way Lenny handled himself before Super Bowl IV," the late Buchanan said. "It inspired all of us."

He was referring to the bogus allegations that NBC broke about Dawson's possible involvement with a Detroit gambler. The allegations were false, and Dawson went on to win the Super Bowl MVP award.

"I actually think some of the pressure from the gambling allegations took away the pressure of the game," Dawson said. "I was there to prepare for a football game and to help my team win a world championship. I think the way I coped with it charged up the guys on the team."

And it made a lasting impression on his teammates.

"Lenny the Cool," Buchanan said, "He was our leader. He was the man."

Added Podolak, "You always had the feeling you were going to win a game because of Lenny. He just made you feel that way, and that's what a leader is supposed to do, isn't it?"

After several snubs, Dawson earned a spot in the Pro Football Hall of Fame in 1987 and true to his nickname, he kept his cool.

"I remember talking to [Hall of Famer] Bobby Mitchell after it was announced that I was going to be inducted and he said, 'Lenny the Cool, I'm going to watch you melt.'"

Not hardly—with the style and grace that personified his career with the Chiefs, Dawson read his induction speech and barely broke a sweat.

"You don't get up here by yourself," he said. "You need an awful lot of help. I was very fortunate."

THE NFL'S FIRST GIANT

Buck Buchanan was a mountain of a man—even by NFL standards. When he enrolled at Grambling to play basketball, he was a 6'7" youngster who tipped the scales at 212 pounds. When he left, he weighed 281 pounds and led the College All-Stars to a stunning upset of the world champion Green Bay Packers in 1963.

"I loved to eat; still do," the late Buchanan said more than a decade ago as he sank his teeth in a mound of pancakes that resembled a mini skyscraper. "Back in college, it was nothing for me to eat six or eight eggs and five or six pieces of toast for breakfast.

"For the longest time, I thought basketball was going to be my sport; then I played football at Grambling and before long, I started to get a lot of attention from pro scouts."

The Dallas Texans won a furious bidding war with the NFL and signed Buchanan with the number one pick in the draft. He proved to be a wise choice as he won two team MVP awards and was a six-time All-AFL player and two-time Pro Bowl pick.

"I didn't feel that much pressure being drafted number one," Buchanan said, "because I had played against some of the best college players in the country and I could hold my own with them.

"There weren't many players as big as I was back in the 1960s and I knew Coach [Hank] Stram was going to make the most of my size and ability. But I kept putting on weight and he was always after me to get into better condition. I played between 286 and 292 pounds.

"I didn't play right away because we had some pretty good defensive linemen—Jerry Mays, Mel Branch, Paul Rochester, and Bobby Bell [who went on to become a Hall of Fame linebacker]. Bell got hurt about five games into the season and Coach put me in at defensive end and I never left."

Buchanan was part of a draft class that also included future Chiefs Ring of Fame members Ed Budde and Bell.

"You knew that we were going to be good; you could just sense it," Buchanan said. "We moved from Dallas to Kansas City my rookie year and it took a while for us to really become a team. We had some great players, and when we became a team, we became a team of champions."

Buchanan was part of the 1966 Chiefs team that walloped Buffalo 31–7 to earn the right to play Green Bay in the first championship game between the two rival leagues.

"That meant a lot to me to play in that game," Buchanan said. "It meant a lot to all the guys. I remember walking down the tunnel to the field before the game. So many people had called us the Mickey Mouse League and said some pretty bad things about us and here we were, ready to play the Green Bay Packers."

Although the Packers claimed a 35–10 victory, Buchanan thought his team could play with the perennial NFL powerhouse.

"Bobby [Bell] and I weren't afraid of them because we'd played on that College All-Star team that beat them in 1963," Buchanan said. "But names like [Vince] Lombardi and [Bart] Starr carried a lot of weight. I don't know—our guys just didn't have a lot of confidence going into that game."

But that all changed two years later when the Chiefs manhandled heavily favored Minnesota 23–7 to win Super Bowl IV.

"We had big defensive games against the Raiders and the Jets to get to the Super Bowl and we were so much bigger than the Vikings. We were all relaxed and confident. We were so dominating in the first half, when Jan [Stenerud] kicked the third field goal and we went up 9–0, we felt like they couldn't come back. Then Otis [Taylor] scores on the long touchdown pass and that was it. It was a great feeling."

Buchanan's emotions flowed following the game.

"I was so proud when the New York Jets beat Baltimore the year before, because an AFL team had beaten an NFL team in the Super Bowl," Buchanan said. "Now, I'm part of an AFL win in the Super Bowl. I remembered the NFL players and coaches calling us Mickey Mouse, and now, it didn't matter. We were the champions."

Perhaps the only thing that surpassed the feeling he experienced following Super Bowl IV came when he was enshrined in the Pro Football Hall of Fame in 1990.

"That was incredible," he said.

By the time of the induction ceremony, Buchanan had begun chemotherapy treatment in his battle against cancer. His body weakened by the disease, he accepted his Hall of Fame ring before a sold-out crowd at Arrowhead Stadium as fellow Chiefs Hall of Famers and former teammates applauded and wiped away tears.

In typical Buchanan fashion, he told the cheering fans, "This belongs to Kansas City."

That was his last appearance at Arrowhead Stadium. He died at the age of 51 on July 16, 1992.

Buchanan's wife, Georgia, who is still active in the community and represents her husband at the annual Chiefs Reunion Game, still remembers the love team owner Lamar Hunt and his wife Norma showed following her husband's death.

"Lamar was on his way to Dallas," Georgia said, "and when he heard about Buck's death, he came to our home for three days. He answered the phone, answered the door, made sure Buck's funeral plans were followed. I'll never forget what he did for our family. He was there when we really needed him."

ONE-OF-A-KIND LINEBACKER

No mention of the greatest players in the history of the NFL would be complete without focusing attention on the first player from the Kansas City Chiefs to be inducted into the Pro Football Hall of Fame.

"I don't know if I ever coached a greater athlete than Bobby Bell," Stram said of the outside linebacker who revolutionized the way the game was played by starring in Stram's famous "stack defense."

"He could do it all. He could throw a football the length of the playing field, outrun most halfbacks, and punt with the best of 'em. He was our long snapper and a standout on special teams. If you wanted to make a highlight reel of how to tackle in the open field, you could use Bobby Bell as a role model."

Bell was an honor student at the University of Minnesota, where he won the Outland Trophy, given to the top interior lineman in the country. At 6'4", 228 pounds, he was small by defensive end standards, but the Chiefs were depleted at that position in 1963 and they used their seventh round pick of the draft to select the future Hall of Famer.

"I didn't know anything about the Chiefs or Kansas City," Bell said. "I know that when Mr. [Lamar] Hunt picked me up at the airport, he didn't have enough money to pay the cabbie and I immediately called my [agent] and asked, 'Did I do the right thing by signing with this team?' Looking back on it, I now know I did the right thing."

So did the Chiefs.

"Bobby was amazing," Dawson said. "They talk about Dick Butkus and Ray Nitschke—and they were great linebackers—but

Bobby Bell, whom Hank Stram called the best athlete he'd ever coached, was one of the greatest linebackers ever to play the game. Photo courtesy of Getty Images.

they weren't any better than Bobby or Willie [Lanier, another Chiefs Hall of Fame linebacker]."

While Bell starred on the field, he would often drive his coach nuts at practice. It wasn't for a lack of effort—no one worked harder than the nine-time AFL and NFL Pro Bowl star. It was because Bell was one of the greatest practical jokers in the history of the team.

"Coach liked to watch practice from this cherry picker," Bell said, laughing at the memory. "He was a short guy and he could see the entire practice field from up there. He'd be yelling at us, and getting on our nerves, so one day he goes up in the picker and I take the distributor cap so it can't come back down."

In a move that was highly unusual for Stram, he congratulated the team on a great practice and said over his loud speaker, "No running today, boys! Great practice!"

Bell was wondering what was going on, and he found out as he walked to the locker room.

"They had [groundskeeper] George Toma out there with this long ladder and Hank was climbing down from the cherry picker," Bell said. "I was laughing so hard I was crying."

The next day, when Bell and his teammates arrived at practice, the cherry picker's inner workings were protected by a couple of padlocks.

"He told me it was my butt if I ever did it again," Bell said, "but that was just the relationship we had. I loved to play practical jokes on him, but I loved playing for him even more."

When Bell strapped on the shoulder pads, he was all business.

"There was a lot of talk back then about why Bobby was playing defense," former Chiefs defensive lineman Mays said. "He would have played tight end, running back, or even wide receiver. He was so fast—I think there were maybe three guys in the league who could outrun him. I know he was faster than [San Diego Hall of Fame wide receiver] Lance Alworth [the first player from the AFL to be inducted into the Pro Football Hall of Fame]."

Bell never cared about his position. His passion for the game was all the fuel he needed to stoke the fires that burned deep within his soul.

"I practiced at safety and cornerback. I was the long snapper. I just wanted to play."

And his 30-inch waistline was the envy of every player at training camp. While they were huffing and puffing their way through two-a-days, Bell was running circles around most of them.

"I didn't drink or smoke," Bell said. "I came into camp in shape. It wasn't hard; it was like vacation. Maybe that's why I always tried to have so much fun with Coach Stram."

Had it not been for one remarkable defensive stand and a defensive gem by Bell, the Chiefs might not have made a return trip to face Minnesota in Super Bowl IV.

The Chiefs opened the 1969 playoffs at Shea Stadium, where they completely shut down Joe Namath and the Jets.

"The one thing I remember about that game," Dawson said, "was that great defensive stand. The Jets have the ball, first down on our 1, and we stopped them. Bobby probably made the biggest play of his career during that stand. We should all thank him every time we look at our [Super Bowl] rings."

Jets fullback Matt Snell gained about half a yard on his first carry and running back Bill Mathis was stopped dead cold on the second running attempt.

"I knew Joe was going to throw a pass because he was such a smart quarterback," Bell said. "He knew he couldn't run against us, so he had to pass the ball."

Namath faked a handoff to Mathis, then rolled out, looking for Snell.

"I'm looking for Snell and all I see is Bell," Namath told Alan Hoskins. "He had no business being there."

With Bell blocking his pass route, Namath had to run for his life. He was tackled by Jim Lynch and the Jets had to settle for a field goal. Kansas City won the game 13–6 and advanced to the AFC Championship Game at Oakland. It turned out to be another defensive masterpiece, with the Chiefs winning 17–7.

After the win over the Jets, Namath approached Bell and good-naturedly asked, "Bell, what were you doing there? You shouldn't have been there." Bell still cackles at the thought of that series, that game, and that comment.

"Those were the days," Bell said. "Those were the days."

While Bell received nearly every award that can be bestowed on a collegiate or professional player, the best came in 1983, when he was inducted into the Pro Football Hall of Fame.

He was the first Chiefs player to receive such recognition. Team owner Lamar Hunt was the first member of the Chiefs family to be inducted into the Canton, Ohio, shrine.

"I never thought I was good enough to make it," Bell said. "I was so surprised when I found out. It was the greatest honor of my life."

And who did he pick as his presenter?

"Coach Stram," he said, smiling. "Who else would I pick?"

JUST CALL HIM "CONTACT"

"Contact." When that happens to be your nickname, you know that you've made an impact on the game of professional football. That's exactly what Hall of Fame middle linebacker Willie Lanier did during a remarkable 11-year career in which he missed only one game and created enough headaches to keep the nation's aspirin manufacturers in business.

"Oh, man, would Willie ever pop people," said fellow Hall of Fame linebacker Bell of his former teammate. "There was just this certain sound when he hit someone. It was like 'Ka-whack!' You didn't even need to see the play, you just knew that Willie had done some damage."

The sound made an impression on former Chiefs All-AFL defensive lineman Mays, who coined Lanier's colorful nickname.

"My first year in Kansas City I followed the style of tackling that we were taught at that time," Lanier said. "You were taught to use your head first and hit players in the middle of their body. It was done in a rather aggressive manner. So, Jerry Mays is the one that I remember that first started calling me 'Contact.'"

Unlike fellow Chiefs Hall of Famers Bell, Buck Buchanan, and Dawson—who mostly played during the glory years at Municipal Stadium—Lanier arrived on the scene in 1967, the year after the Chiefs lost the first Super Bowl.

"I missed the first Super Bowl by a season," Lanier said, "but I was part of Super Bowl IV and will never forget the feeling after that game. I'm not an emotional person, but the emotions were flowing after we beat the Vikings. It was the last time an AFL club would ever play an NFL club, because of the merger, and we felt like we were playing for the entire league."

Like so many of his teammates, he wonders what might have happened had the Chiefs found a way to win the Christmas Day playoff game in 1971 against the Miami Dolphins.

"We lost that game and you could see that we weren't the same team the next few years. We lost to Miami in the first game at Arrowhead Stadium the next year and went 8–6. We just didn't have the horses we had back in the mid-1960s through the 1970s."

He also admits that he missed the fan-friendly confines of Municipal Stadium, where the Chiefs ruled the AFL.

"We were never 2–12 at Municipal Stadium," laments Lanier (who was part of two 12-loss Chiefs teams in the mid-1970s). "Those were different times, but there was something special about playing at Municipal Stadium. We only played there—we didn't practice there—so when you walked out on the field on a Sunday afternoon, it was special. The fans were cheering, the players were ready to go, and it just felt comfortable, like you were at home."

Opposing offensive players never felt at home when No. 63 was staring them down from across the line.

Willie Lanier was known for his ferocious hits on opposing ball carriers. Photo courtesy of Getty Images.

14

"I'm glad I never had to play against him," Dawson said, chuckling. "He was something to see. Just think, at one time we had two Hall of Fame linebackers in Bobby and Willie and they just overshadowed poor Jim Lynch, who probably should be in the Hall of Fame, too."

While Lanier was the face of the Chiefs defense following the retirement of Bell, Buchanan, Mays, and so many other former All-Pro players, he admitted to *Football Digest* that it became difficult to get up for opponents when the Chiefs were struggling (they were just 14–27–1 at Arrowhead Stadium during his career).

"When you're winning, it's a lot easier to play. It's a lot easier to develop confidence because you know the odds are with you. If you go out on the field and there's one of you and 10 of them, it's a little more difficult to be enthusiastic about your chances."

It was also difficult for Lanier to deal with the mediocrity that had become commonplace at Arrowhead Stadium.

"You can't minimize losing," he said. "When we were 12–2 and in the playoffs rather than 2–12, playing football was a lot more fun."

Ironically, he and Lynch both retired following the 1977 season, and their final game was against the hated Raiders, a 21–20 Oakland victory.

"We all hated Oakland," Lanier said, a thin smile appearing on his face, "but we loved to play them. Raiders games—especially during the early years—were always something special. We only beat them once in Oakland, but that game really meant something."

It was a 17–7 victory that sent the Chiefs to Super Bowl IV.

"We beat the New York Jets the week before, 13–6, and beat the Raiders 17–7—and then beat the Vikings 23–7," Lanier said. "Our defense allowed a total of 20 points against two of the best teams in the AFL and the best team in the NFL. You take a lot of pride in being a part of something like that."

You don't hear Lanier talk about his personal accomplishments (and there are many of them): two AFL All-Star starts, six NFL Pro Bowl appearances, a Hall of Fame ring, and being named to the NFL's 75th Anniversary All-Time Team.

But the one honor he will talk about is being named the NFL Man of the Year in 1972 for his work with Kansas City's drug abuse campaign.

"That was the greatest honor I could imagine," Lanier said. "It was bigger than the Super Bowl. Just seven years earlier I was in college and now, a $25,000 scholarship had been awarded in my name. It gives five young people the chance to go to school and make something out of their lives."

Lanier will always remember his relationship with his former coach and teammates.

"It was wonderful playing for Hank because of his winning record and his positive attitude," Lanier said. "He put together the best group of players that could compete and show the kind of confidence that he did.

"The benefits of playing—the games won and lost, the championships, the trophies, the yellow press clippings—are all temporary. But the friendships are the things that last forever."

Friendships, and the sound of No. 63 ripping into an opposing running back or tight end.

Ka-whack!

Perhaps the greatest compliment Lanier ever received came from another pretty decent linebacker—Dick Butkus, the former Chicago Bears great who is considered by many to be the standard by which every other player is measured. When attending a celebrity golf tournament in Kansas City, Butkus was asked about Lanier.

"I once heard someone refer to Willie Lanier as the 'Black Butkus,'" Butkus said, rolling a foot-long cigar around his mouth. "That's an insult to Willie Lanier. He was as good as anyone who ever played that position."

HE KICKED HIS WAY INTO THE HALL OF FAME

Curiosity got the best of a visiting football coach at old Municipal Stadium. He simply couldn't figure out what all the white X markings were on the wall that was 10 yards behind the goal post in the west end zone. Finally he asked groundskeeper Toma about the strange markings.

Toma just smiled and said, "Those are the spots where Stenerud's kickoffs have hit the fence."

The coach just shook his head and went about his pregame routine, knowing that Jan Stenerud would likely play a key role in another Chiefs victory.

Stenerud's path to the Chiefs is stranger than fiction. The only true place-kicker in the Pro Football Hall of Fame came to the United States from Norway after earning an athletic scholarship at Montana State University.

The scholarship wasn't for soccer or field hockey—two games Stenerud played as a youngster—it was for ski jumping. Stenerud never imagined appearing in a Super Bowl, but his parents dreamed of him competing in the Winter Olympics.

"I was on the ski team and part of the workout was always running the stadium steps at Montana State," Stenerud said. "And while the ski team would run the stadium steps, a couple of the football players would kick extra points down on the field. And I went down and kicked a few with the toe, like everybody kicked it in those days. And I asked them if I could kick with the side of my foot, like they take a corner kick in soccer, and they said 'Yes, yes, you can.' So I started kicking a few with the side of my foot."

Montana State basketball coach Roger Craft was watching this sophomore ski jumper bomb kick after kick, so he sought out football coach Jim Sweeney.

"Coach Sweeney saw me a couple of weeks later running the stadium steps and he hollered at me and said, 'Hey, get down here. Hear you can kick.' So I kicked a few in front of the team. And they thought I had a chance, and they decided I should go out for spring practice. So I went out for spring practice my senior year and made the team."

Not only did he make the team, he made collegiate history by kicking what was then the longest NCAA field goal ever (59 yards).

Stenerud kicked 18 of 33 field goals in two seasons at MSU. His percentage might have been better if Sweeney had a reliable punter. The coach would often send Stenerud in to attempt an impossible kick, rather than punt the ball a few yards down the field. Stenerud might be the only kicker in the history of the

NCAA to attempt an 113-yard field goal that sailed to the opponent's 30-yard line.

But even before Stenerud attempted a field goal for the Bobcats, he actually witnessed a Chiefs game in person. Before he enrolled at Montana State in 1963, Stenerud visited his sister, Berit, who was dating a Buffalo sportswriter named Larry Felser. He asked Stenerud and his sister if they would like to attend a football game. The Chiefs were going to play the Buffalo Bills.

Stenerud still recalls his reaction to that AFL contest.

"It's the craziest thing," Stenerud said. "I can't understand why all those guys keep jumping on top of each other."

The Chiefs and Bills might have been jumping on top of each other, but it was Chiefs coach Stram who was jumping for joy when he heard about the Norwegian ski-jumper-turned-kicker.

"We drafted Jan as a future choice in 1966," Stram said, "but I wanted to see the kid in person so I went to see a game in Tulsa.

Jan Stenerud dominated the kicking game to the degree that rule changes had to be made, much as Wilt Chamberlain did in the NBA.

On the opening kickoff, he put the ball through the goal posts and seven rows deep into the bleachers. I had seen all I needed to see."

Stenerud signed with the Chiefs and, 19 years later, would retire as the most prolific and successful kicker in the history of the game.

"Now, what you have to remember about Jan is that back then, special teams guys didn't get much practice," said Chiefs quarterback Dawson, who held for Stenerud on field goals. "There weren't any domed stadiums or kicking nets to practice with on the sidelines. This guy was way, way ahead of his time.

"I think he kicked a 54-yarder in the first game against Houston and we all thought we really had something special."

That year Stenerud kicked what was then a team record of 21 field goals. That total also led the AFL. Stenerud always gave credit to Stram, who made sure the newcomer to football felt at ease and appreciated.

"Coach brought me in a month early before my first season," Stenerud says. "Every day he had me out there kicking 50 balls, and he was doing all the holding. It was Coach Stram who pointed out that I was more likely to miss a field goal from the right hash mark. I didn't realize that, but his charts showed me it was true. He had me practice from that side until it was no longer a problem."

After his first AFL season, Stenerud returned to Norway to visit his family. He brought some game film so they could see what the football thing was all about, but their reaction was much the same to his after he saw the Chiefs and Bills play three years earlier.

"My mother was a little leery of my playing football," Stenerud said, "and my father hoped I would jump for Norway in the Winter Olympics. And when they looked at the film, nobody could understand what was happening."

What was happening was a revolution in pro football. Much like the way Wilt Chamberlain revolutionized basketball (several rule changes were enacted to harness the ability of the 7'1" giant, including widening the lane, instituting offensive goaltending, and revising rules governing inbounding the ball), Stenerud was dominating the game of pro football.

Because his kickoffs were sailing into the stands, the line from which the ball was kicked was moved from the 40 to the 35, and eventually to the 30. But nothing could stop Stenerud, whose career achievements are made even more impressive by the fact that he played the game before coaches even began thinking about positioning a kicker to make a key field goal in a game.

He scored 1,699 points and held the career record with 373 successful field goals, 38 more than former leader George Blanda. Stenerud was tied with his Chiefs predecessor, Nick Lowery, with seven seasons scoring over 100 points. In 1969 he kicked 16 straight field goals, eclipsing the existing pro mark of 13 straight held by Cleveland's Hall of Fame tackle Lou Groza. He ranked second with 17 field goals over 50 yards—his longest was a 55-yarder against Denver in 1970. His 580 career points after touchdown place him third in that category.

The personable kicker played in two AFL All-Star Games and four AFC-NFC Pro Bowls. With four field goals, including a then-record 48-yarder, and two extra points, he was named the Most Valuable Offensive Player in the 1972 Pro Bowl. From 1967 to 1970 he was successful on 72 percent of his field-goal attempts, while the AFL average during the same time was just over 51 percent.

"If Jan were playing today," Dawson said, "there is no telling what he could do."

While he was a teenager in Norway, Stenerud had no idea what the Super Bowl was all about. But he made it his own personal stage when the Chiefs defeated Minnesota 23–7 in Super Bowl IV.

Stenerud got the Chiefs on the scoreboard with a then–Super Bowl record 48-yard effort. He followed with 32- and 25-yarders and gave the Chiefs a 9–0 first-half lead. Mike Garrett followed with a short touchdown run and suddenly the Chiefs led 16–0 at the half.

"At halftime, we had the lead," Stenerud said, "and we're half an hour away from the world championship. And because of all the halftime activities, it lasted twice as long as a normal halftime.

It seemed 10 times as long. I remember that clearly, and how strange that was. We had the momentum going, but when we went out there, it was almost like starting a new game."

The Vikings never got their running game on track and the Chiefs knocked out quarterback Joe Kapp, claiming their first Super Bowl triumph.

"I remember the total elation when the game was over," he said. "I am not one to scream and yell. If the 75,000 fans were like me, you would hardly hear a sound. But it was a terrific feeling of accomplishment. And I also remember thinking about the other guys who had played for so long in the AFL. To beat the old league in the last game between the two leagues, I know how terrific it felt for them."

Stenerud didn't feel as good following his next big game, a postseason loss to the Miami Dolphins two seasons later in a Christmas Day contest in which he missed a possibly game-winning 32-yard field goal in the fourth quarter. He then had another field goal blocked in overtime, and the Dolphins went on to claim a two-overtime 27–24 win that Stenerud will never forget.

"To this day, I don't know how I missed that field goal," he said. "I hit it firm and well. Everything was perfect."

Nine years after that missed field goal, the Chiefs did what many fans considered the unthinkable.

"Hank was gone and Marv Levy was coaching the team and he never liked the way I kicked," Stenerud said, "so they released me. He was new, he wanted his own team and a younger guy, so they took Nick Lowery over me."

That move meant that Stenerud would be the first member of the Chiefs' small fraternity of Pro Football Hall of Famers who would finish their careers outside of Kansas City.

Following his release in 1980, Stenerud signed a free-agent contract to play the last four games with the Green Bay Packers. The next year he beat out two veteran kickers and his 91.7 completion percentage on 22 of 24 attempts was the finest of his career.

In 1983 he won or tied five games in the last two minutes and broke Blanda's career field-goal mark with four field goals in a 12–9 Monday night win over Tampa Bay.

Stenerud was traded to the Minnesota Vikings for a seventh-round draft pick the following year and the veteran was excited about playing in a domed stadium for the first time in his career.

He connected on 20 of 23 field goals for an 87 percent success rate, and at the age of 42, he became the oldest player ever to participate in the Pro Bowl.

Stenerud scored 86 points on 15 of 26 field goals and 41 extra points in his final NFL season. A bad back that continued to cause him pain before and after games then forced him to say good-bye to pro football.

In his first year of eligibility, the former ski jumping champion became the first pure place-kicker inducted into the Hall of Fame.

"I know that when I got a note that I was one of the 15 finalists, I knew I was in a position that nobody has been in before," he said. "So I didn't know what to expect at all. It was total uncharted territory. I got enough votes the first time I was eligible and I thought it was very exciting and was very proud of it."

AN UNLIKELY HALL OF FAMER

When you have a Hall of Famer of Norwegian descent who came to the United States on a ski jumping scholarship, you might be hard pressed to find a more unlikely member of the elite football fraternity.

But in Kansas City, you need look no further than the first member of the Chiefs family to gain Hall of Fame recognition. He was a quiet and polite former third-string wide receiver from Southern Methodist University who initially was known in the Dallas area as the son of one of the richest men in the world. That was before 26-year-old Lamar Hunt formed "the Foolish Club" and founded the American Football League.

Hunt's father was H.L. Hunt, who had an income of more than $1 million per week when he ruled the oil game in Texas.

The elder Hunt was not a fan of professional sports endeavors, but the old man had a sense of humor. When someone told him that Lamar's Dallas Texans had lost $1 million, he quipped, "At that rate, they will last only 100 years!"

Just 10 years after the birth of Hunt's new league, the AFL merged with the more established NFL, and today football has replaced baseball as America's game.

The world of sports may never produce another visionary like Hunt, who garnered so much respect from his peers. In fact the hunk of hardware the American Football Conference champion wins is called the Lamar Hunt Trophy. He came up with the name "Super Bowl" to represent the NFL's championship game and brought countless industries, including Worlds of Fun, to the Kansas City metro area.

He may be gone after losing a long battle with prostate cancer in 2006, but his ideals will live forever.

When he became the first member of the AFL to be enshrined in the Hall of Fame, it would have offered the perfect opportunity to thumb his nose at all those individuals who said the AFL was a joke, the poor stepsister of the NFL.

But that wasn't Hunt's style.

"I'm the last person to claim personal justification," he said. "My selection is symbolic of all the general managers, coaches, and players who worked for the growth of the American Football League."

Nothing gave Hunt more pleasure than talking about the AFL, whether it was over the phone from his Dallas office or home or in his tasteful suite at Arrowhead Stadium. He had told the stories many times over, but his enthusiastic approach made the listener believe this was the first time his thoughts had been made public.

His thoughts of forming a new league started back in 1958, when he tried to convince Walter Wolfner, who owned the Chicago Cardinals, to move the struggling franchise to Dallas.

"There were 12 NFL teams back then, and I talked to Walter about moving the team. He wasn't interested, but he did offer to sell 20 percent of the team. That's not what I was looking for. I wanted a team in Dallas. But he also said something that caught my attention. He said there were many individuals making inquiries about buying the team."

Hunt thought that a new league might be the answer to his question, especially if there were other individuals out there who were trying to buy a franchise.

"In early 1959 I began to contact other people," he said. "The first was Bud Adams in Houston. I felt it was important to have a Dallas-Houston rivalry. We had six people, five plus myself, who were interested in a new league if I could put it together.

"In early August, I called them and scheduled our first organizational meeting in Chicago. It was the first time they had met each other. They all got along nicely, for the time being anyway."

Hunt eventually found eight other men who were willing to put up the money to own a team, and in 1960 the American Football League was born.

"There were a couple of times that first season that I didn't know if we would make it," Hunt admitted. "I got a call from Bob Howsam, the Denver owner, who said he wasn't sure if they would be able to finish the season. But they survived, and so did the league.

"In 1962 the New York Titans were struggling and had to be supported by the league. We needed a strong franchise in New York and they were the worst. The turning point came when Sonny Werblin and his group took over the franchise the next year. We then signed a big TV deal, Sonny signed Joe Namath to a big contract, and the league began to take off."

The early days of the AFL had a cloak-and-dagger feel, like the time the Chiefs coaxed a youngster from Prairie View A&M to climb out of a hotel window so they could sign him away from the Dallas Cowboys.

"It was a fantastically exciting era," Hunt said. "From 1960 to 1966 it was the battle over players, like when we had to sneak Otis Taylor out of the window of a motel room. There were lawsuits over Billy Cannon and Jimmy Robinson. There were the big contract offers to Namath and others.

"Otis was a senior out of Prairie View A&M, and the Dallas Cowboys were babysitting him in a motel room to keep him away from the AFL scouts back in 1964. But one of our scouts, Lloyd Welles, went into the motel and found a janitor to give a message to Otis. Otis climbed out the window of the motel, got into Lloyd's car, and was on the next flight to Kansas City. We signed him the next day."

Players like Taylor, Dawson, Buchanan, and Bell made the AFL a legitimate league. And before long, their weekend heroics were televised nationally.

"Television was the big factor," Hunt said when asked about the growth of the league. "We got an ABC-TV contract the first year. It didn't pay much the first five years, but at least we were on the network.

"One of the key games was the 1962 championship between the Texans and Oilers. We won the game in six quarters. We had an advantage because there was no other game on television that day and there was bad weather around the country. We had a tremendous audience."

It was an audience that Hunt could never envision back in the early days of the Chiefs, when 6,200 people were showing up for games.

"No way," he said. "We couldn't conceptualize what has happened, especially with the television. No one believed the numbers would be as high as they are. Not to steal baseball's title, but we have become the national pastime. People build their schedules around *Monday Night Football*. It's silly to say we knew it would become this big."

HOW IT ALL BEGAN

IN LAMAR HUNT'S WORDS

Imagine being there and having an eyewitness account of the start of professional baseball, football, or basketball. Because those sports have been around for decades, that is not possible. But because of his insight and forethought, Lamar Hunt, sat down and wrote an intricate account of how the American Football League came about. Here, in his own words, are his thoughts on the birth of the AFL.

How did the AFL start? You never think of a lightbulb coming on, but that was it, exactly, just like an old cartoon. The light just clicked on and got brighter and brighter.

It occurred to me, "Hey, what would be the possibility of putting together a second league?" I had had a number of conversations with the Wolfners [Mrs. Wolfner owned the Chicago Cardinals team]. In the course of these conversations, they ultimately agreed to sell 20 percent of the team, but they didn't want it to move out of Chicago. They would let me have an option that if they ever moved, that they would move to Dallas.

It really wasn't something I wanted to do. In the course of the conversation, they had mentioned many individuals' names. Did I know Bud Adams in Houston, Bob Howsam in Denver, Max Winter or Bill Boyer in Minneapolis?

It turns out these were all people who had come to them about buying the Cardinals and moving them to their town. I thought about those people, and that's when the lightbulb went off. If all of those people are interested, why not get them all together and form a league?

Never had a turndown. [Surprised] Knowing what I know now, I would expect some turndowns. The original six people we approached, no one turned us down.

We were called "the Foolish Club." Wayne Valley came up with that one day. He said, "This is a really foolish group. We ought to call ourselves the Foolish Club." He said he was going to start calling us "the Foolish Club." Soon, everyone started calling us that.

When the league was announced, I was a few days away from 27. If I knew then what I know now, I would be on the beach at Waikiki, and not involved in a league. It was a different time and a different era. Now there are so many things that have gone on in sports expansion: teams failing, the ABA, WHA, even some of the NHL is failing. Obviously there was the WFL. That was a very naïve time, thinking that it would be fairly easy to start a new league, that if it would succeed in Pittsburgh, Cleveland, and Washington, why won't it succeed in Dallas, Houston, and Denver?

What made the AFL different from the ABA, WHA, WFL? I think we were an idea whose time was right. Football had come into a success era—the NFL. There was a pattern there with baseball, with two leagues. There was a void there.

All we really wanted to do was copy a successful format. Unless we made real bad business decisions, we really should have been able to make it succeed. We were lucky in the choice of people. The way some of them came about is just amazing.

Ralph Wilson wrote me a letter in the mail. I kid him about being a mail-order franchise. He just wrote a letter. He had heard about the league. He was a minority stockholder in the Lions; he was interested in a team in Miami. Today, he is still 100 percent owner. Bud Adams, Ralph Wilson, myself—we had an ownership continuity that lasted a long, long time. Up until about five years ago, there was an ownership tie with every original team except one, the Titans.

There were minor ownership changes. A team like Oakland had eight or nine partners the first year, and there was some shakeout the next—Ed McGah, Barron Hilton. Phipps sold out four years ago, five years ago in Denver. New England, Bill Sullivan headed the original group of 10 people at 10 percent each, except for two years, when he was forced out and then he came back and bought the other people out. New York made a complete change, but even there they have had the same ownership for 22 years. We have had a lot of continuity, even more so than the average, old NFL teams.

Representatives of the new American Football League pose in a football-like formation in New York City on October 28, 1959. Posing in the front row, from left, are Robert L. Howsam, Denver; Max Winter, Minneapolis–St. Paul; league founder Lamar Hunt, Dallas; and K.S. Adams Jr., Houston. In the back row are, from left, Barron Hilton, Los Angeles; Ralph C. Wilson Jr., Buffalo; and Harry Wismer, New York.

That continuity helped. The financial continuity helped. We had three 100 percent owners. We are all actively involved in the recruiting process. I don't think you see that today in sports; it is much more complicated today. Bud Adams really worked at player recruiting; that is something he loved. He didn't mind that it might cost a few more dollars. It meant keeping another player away from the NFL. I know I didn't have one single thing on paper. I didn't have a typed proposal, demographics, or television markets. I thought demographics was a Yugoslav basketball player.

I described it pretty much as I did to you. I told these people I had been to see the Cardinals, that I wanted to see a team in Dallas. It occurred to me that another league might make a go of it. I heard [their] names as interested in the Cardinals.

The NFL was not going to expand, and I thought maybe a second league would be of interest. The conversation was basically very simple. They were pretty short conversations, a couple of hours. Bud Adams took me to dinner. There really wasn't any sales pitch. The numbers were very reasonable. We weren't looking for $6 million.

We were asking each team to put up $25,000, which would be the league treasury. We were naïve to think that would last very long. There were no premonitions in it. It was ready to happen. I think we were lucky to find people who were good football fans and could financially make a commitment. Only exception was Bob Howsam. He was a baseball man. Denver was a city that I happened to believe had great potential. He owned the stadium there for his minor league baseball team. His era lasted just a year, but there was continuity with minor partners.

Another exception was Harry Wismer, who was underfinanced. He was a stockholder in two NFL teams before the AFL. He owned 25 percent of the Redskins and he owned 4 percent of the Lions in a trust. We required him to sell out to go into the AFL venture. Staying together, and keeping enough financial stability that all survived, there were no wholesale dropouts as happened in other leagues.

We nationalized—that's the wrong word—we helped make the game national. It was basically a Northern game before. One thing I put on paper—have you ever seen my map of America? You can take a map of the state of Texas, and lay it over the top of all 10 of these cities. It showed that the game could go national. Instead of the game being concentrated in the Northeast, the AFL overnight took it to Denver, Dallas, Houston, and Minneapolis. Whole parts of the country with enormous populations did not have pro football.

The AFL really triggered that. It would not have happened nearly that fast without the AFL. It was happening at a snail's pace, sort of like it is now. That was a minor accomplishment. It wasn't the goal we set out with. My interest was seeing Dallas get a team, the Dallas-Houston tie, and so on.

One of the most significant things was Sonny Werblin's purchase of the Titans. That took our very weakest links and, almost overnight, they became one of the strongest ownership groups in the most important media market in the country. Instead of our being the laughingstock there, almost immediately we had the upper hand, because Sonny had such great manner and image with the media. Just a year later, Shea Stadium was completed. By the second year at Shea, they were selling out. It was a very rapid turnaround.

I personally favored the league moving the team out of New York. We had a chance to sell to somebody in Miami, and I didn't think it was worth staying in New York, playing at the Polo Grounds in front of 5,000 people. I was very shortsighted. I didn't know how strong a guy Sonny could be. Sonny was the guy who got us our second television contract, and that would have to be another very, very important moment, the five-year deal we signed with NBC in February of 1964. My wife Norma and I were on our honeymoon in Innsbrook at the Olympics.

Ralph Wilson was there [in New York] and more in touch with what was happening. Sonny, through his friendships, succeeded in making us equal to the NFL from a monetary standpoint. We only had eight teams. You can imagine if that happened today and somebody came forward and paid the USFL equal money to what we are getting, they would have it made. That was a key.

The good fortune [was] with the original ownership group; I had no idea how lucky this was, but we didn't end up with a lot of fractionalized ownership. New England had 10 people with 10 percent each. Every new league seems to have that kind of problem. Joe Namath, the great player, was really a public relations creation of Werblin. If you remember that year, he signed two quarterbacks—Namath and John Huarte, who won the Heisman Trophy. He signed them the same season. Namath had the arm, too. They had $41,000 paid the year before Namath played in their first year at Shea Stadium. Second year, they averaged $58,000, which was essentially capacity. PR wise, the public saw that as one of the very key things.

Only thing I had against Sonny, he wanted us to leave Kansas City. In 1965–66, he wanted us to get out of Denver and KC, and get into Philadelphia and Chicago. George Blanda did, not so much early. He became sort of a folk hero when he started doing the field goals and quarterbacking.

Early on there were other stars, like Billy Cannon, clearly. I think Keith Lincoln was great. He had a great championship game performance. Ernie Ladd was another great player, for the Chargers. Kansas City players through the late 1970s were the best. It was ironic—hard to look back on now and say, [but] the AFL did not develop its own quarterbacks right away. The people who came into our league and did well were Blanda, Len Dawson, and Namath, one of the first rookie players that came out of college and did well in the AFL. And John Hadl did. We developed a lot of good players early out of college because we had the ability and aggressiveness to sign players to not too big a financial commitment. Our first year we signed Jack Spikes, and I think we gave him a thousand dollars more than Pittsburgh was offering. I think it is a very different situation [now]. I think we hit a market where it was ready to happen, when the map was ready to expand. There are cities now that would like pro football. There are a bunch of them: Phoenix, Memphis, Birmingham. Those cities are the minority, and are least important in their picture.

They've got to succeed in the big television markets, because it is a television league. We didn't have to succeed in the big markets, except we felt we wanted a team in New York and Los Angeles 25 years ago. That was part of the verbal train of thought. The difference now is that they had a lot better stadium situation than we did. We couldn't get into Miami because the city of Miami wouldn't rent the Orange Bowl to a pro team. We couldn't go into Seattle. We had a guy who wanted to have an original team, but we couldn't get the University of Washingtons's stadium. We couldn't get Tulane Stadium in New Orleans. Today, they can get just about any stadium they want. And there are more stadiums around today.

Almost as soon as he signed with the AFL, a player was maligned, and asked, "Why did you do something dumb like that?" People don't seem to ask that question today. In those days, the party line was so hammered out by the NFL, that this was an inferior league and so on, there was almost a battle that developed ideologically between old NFL cities. They didn't even report the scores. That atmosphere probably exists today in places like Birmingham and Memphis, places where they don't have NFL teams.

Togetherness would be in my top five. They helped each other in recruiting. I can remember making phone calls on behalf of Oakland, trying to get them players, if you can believe that. Lance Alworth, I made a pitch for him. He signed with the Chargers, signed with the league. It was to our own benefit. It was almost unthinkable for a player to jump leagues. Willard Deuveall did and, after that happened, we established a policy that we weren't interested in signing any NFL veterans. As opposed to now, when the first thing you do is go out and raid somebody. There was a pride. I always think of Jerry Mays. It used to make him so mad.

I can't tell you how much we didn't want to buy the Cowboys. Taking it national, the two leagues heightened the interest in both leagues, created the Super Bowl, the number one event in America today. If the NFL had expanded on a normal schedule of two teams every four or five years, I don't know how many teams they would have. They would still be playing an East and West championship. There never would have been a Super Bowl created. It is hard to believe anything as archaic as that.

It was a pretty big business then, too. It was darn important to me. I had a lot of money in it, a lot invested in it. Emotionally it was something I spent a lot of time, effort, and energy on. I felt the obligation. For Bill Sullivan, he had everything he had in it.

When we started, NFL teams were thought to be worth $1 million or $2 million. Bud Adams has been quoted as saying he put $1 million in the bank to purchase the Cardinals and he lost about $2 million after about five years.

My, how things have changed.

THEY WEREN'T SO FOOLISH AFTER ALL

"THE FOOLISH CLUB" AND THE AFL

The American Football League.

"It's nice to hear those words," Chiefs Hall of Fame linebacker Bobby Bell said. "A lot of people have forgotten about the old AFL. I mean, there aren't many of us left who played in the AFL. Just in the past year, we lost Hank [Chiefs coach Hank Stram] and Lamar [Chiefs and AFL founder Lamar Hunt] and a lot of the guys I played with and against are gone. But as long as there are a few of us around, it will never be forgotten."

In visions of wavy black and white Motorola television screens or grainy newspaper photos that are yellowed and dog-eared, the AFL comes to life. John Hadl throws a perfect spiral to the league's greatest receiver, Lance "Bambi" Alworth, as a disgruntled Emmitt Thomas looks on; ol' man George Blanda plods out on the field to throw a miracle touchdown pass or kick a game-winning field goal for the hated Oakland Raiders; "Broadway" Joe Namath, the most charismatic player in the history of the league, barely flips his wrist to throw a perfect strike to fellow Hall of Famer Don Maynard as he streaks down the sideline for a touchdown; monstrous Ernie Ladd moves like no other 300-pound man on the planet and grabs Oakland's Daryle Lamonica by the back of the shoulder pads and flips him to the turf with no more effort than he uses to fluff a pillow.

"That's the AFL," Dawson said. "It was a great league, a league that offered explosive football and high-scoring games. I know the coaches and players in the NFL looked down on us, but look at what happened after 10 years. There was a merger, we won two of the first four Super Bowls, and we finally got some respect."

Dawson paused for a moment, and added with a solemn tone to his voice, "I just hope Mr. Hunt realizes how many lives he changed. It if weren't for Lamar, I'd have never come to Kansas City. I'd been riding the bench in Cleveland and Pittsburgh for five years and was never going to get the chance to play, and he gave me the chance to prove that I belonged in the league. There are a lot of people who owe him a big thank you, but he was such a humble guy, he never looked at it that way. He just wanted to form a new league so he could have some fun and own a football team. I was never around anyone who loved the game as much as he did."

Hunt, who passed away in 2006 following a long bout with prostate cancer, was the son of Texas billionaire H.L. Hunt. As a 27-year-old man sitting on the edge of his bed in a Houston hotel room, Lamar watched the Baltimore Colts' overtime win over the New York Giants in what many experts call the NFL's greatest game.

DID YOU KNOW...

Warpaint, a pinto horse that rider Bob Johnson rode around the playing field following every Chiefs touchdown, was the team's first mascot. On one occasion at old Municipal Stadium, Johnson coaxed the dapper bandleader Tony DiPardo to jump behind him for a touchdown lap. "It was the first time in my life I was ever on a horse," DiPardo said, "and I was scared to death." The first Warpaint, who died at the age of 37 and is buried at Benjamin Stables, was replaced by the cartoon-like KC Wolf in 1989. KC Wolf battles evildoers dressed in gear worn by the Chiefs' opponent that day in a pre-game skit that opens every home game.

That game was a turning point in the NFL because it was televised and created such a stir that the league soon became the talk of the nation. It was also a turning point in Hunt's life because at that moment, he thought about starting his own league.

"I loved it, and I wanted to be involved," Hunt said. "I spent the next few months talking to businessmen about starting a new league, asking them if they'd be interested in a new league if I could find six or seven other willing partners. We got six together pretty quickly, and by the summer of 1959, we were able to make our announcement that the AFL would commence playing in 1960.

"From there, we went on to have our first draft in November of 1959, and then came the business of putting together football teams in all of our eight cities. Nobody really knew what we were doing. None of us had ever been in the football business before, so we were just going by instinct. It was as far from the way things are done today as you can imagine."

The roster of original AFL owners, who often referred to themselves as members of "the Foolish Club," included Ralph Wilson in Buffalo, Billy Sullivan in Boston, Bob Howsam in Denver, Bud Adams in Houston, Barron Hilton in Los Angeles, Max Winter in Minneapolis-St. Paul, Harry Wismer in New York, and Hunt in Dallas. Before the 1960 season, Winter pulled out of his AFL commitment in Minneapolis when the NFL voted to expand to the Twin Cities. The AFL replaced Minnesota with Oakland and a group headed by Chet Soda.

War hero Joe Foss was named the league's first commissioner, but it was Hunt who quietly ran the league. He kept in touch with the other members of "the Foolish Club" and bankrolled the league until it began making some money. Hunt even negotiated the league's first contract with ABC.

The ABC deal was based on advertising sales and eventually paid each team $112,000 during the 1960 season—a miniscule amount compared to today's million-dollar deals that assure each team of staying in the black. At the time, the NFL let each team negotiate its own TV deal and, in some cases, the AFL teams received more money than their established counterparts.

JUST CALL HIM "PSYCHO"

Whenever members of the Kansas City Chiefs reunite for the annual Reunion Game at Arrowhead Stadium, the stories from the good ol' days always dominate the conversation.

Players remember the days when they hung their street clothes on nails in the visiting locker rooms, had to shower back at the hotel following a game, or even did their own laundry.

The tales are as wild and colorful as the men who tell them. When you get a group of former players together, it is often tough to get them to agree on anything—except this one item: when asked who the toughest player to ever wear a Chiefs uniform was, the answer is unanimous.

"Sherrill Headrick is the toughest SOB on the planet," said former center and linebacker E.J. Holub, who is also among the toughest players in team history.

"Mr. Sherrill Headrick," added quarterback Dawson. "One game Sherrill broke a finger and the bone is sticking through the skin. He tells the team doctor to tape it up with a Popsicle stick as a brace and he goes back in on the next series. His nickname was Psycho, and he earned it."

"Sherrill has no concern for his physical safety in a game," Chiefs coach Stram told the Associated Press. "He is a great competitor."

Headrick never misses a reunion game and arrives in a wheelchair, as his body is ravaged by the wear and tear of nine years in the AFL.

"I don't regret one thing," Headrick said.

When asked about his most serious injury, he shrugs and says, "I broke my neck in the warm-ups before we played Houston. I didn't even know my neck was broken until five days later, when it started to hurt and I got X-rays. That game against Houston was one of my best."

The AFL averaged 16,000 fans a game that first year and Blanda led the Houston Oilers to the first championship when they beat the Los Angeles Chargers 24–16. Former Heisman Trophy winner Billy Cannon was one of Blanda's favorite receivers.

While the offenses in the AFL lit up scoreboards across the country like Christmas trees, there were still doubters—and most of them could be found in cities that housed NFL teams.

"We knew what people were saying," Dawson said, "how we were an inferior league. I remember sitting in a team meeting with the Cleveland Browns and Paul Brown started talking about the AFL and what a bad league it was and how a bunch of 'sons of millionaires who don't know anything about football' owned the teams. Well, I'd been sitting on the bench for a long time, and that league sounded pretty good to me."

It also sounded pretty good to Otis Taylor, a former Chiefs number four draft pick from Prairie View, Texas, who teamed with Dawson to become the most famous offensive duo in the Chiefs' AFL history.

"We all liked offense back then," Taylor said, "and the AFL was all about offense. I think one of the big reasons we were so successful was because Coach Stram also believed in having a great defense. With our defense and our offense, we were pretty tough to beat. Just ask the Minnesota Vikings [the NFL team the Chiefs stunned 23–7 in Super Bowl IV]."

Hunt believed there was only one way this new league could survive.

"We had to make sure that each team was successful," said Hunt, who moved his unsuccessful franchise from Dallas to Kansas City in 1963. Three years later the Chiefs were the AFL champions and were gearing up to play the Green Bay Packers in the first AFL-NFL World Championship Game.

"I wanted to play good, competitive football, and I wanted the Chiefs to win," Hunt explained. "The key was making sure we improved every year, because that represented progress. But I was just as happy to see the Jets sign a top draft choice or the Bills do the same, because as each team got better, it made the whole league stronger. It wouldn't have made sense if we made ourselves into a super team while our partners were languishing. We all had to make progress in order to strengthen ourselves."

Curt Gowdy, the legendary voice of the AFL in those early years who died from cancer in 2006 at the age of 86, was a big fan of what Hunt and the other AFL owners were trying to accomplish.

"In the early years, everybody knew the [AFL] football was inferior to the NFL," Gowdy told *Pro Football Weekly*. "But it was exciting, offensive football and it got better every year. We knew the NFL was laughing, but we also knew that AFL football was able to stand on its own and do it a lot faster than anyone thought it could. All that laughing did was solidify the AFL and make sure everyone had a league-wide perspective."

Blanda and his Oilers downed the Chargers in the first two AFL Championship Games, but it was the new league's third title contest that attracted national attention. Hunt's Texans downed the Oilers 20–17 in two overtimes that ended when Tommy Brooker kicked a 25-yard field goal after an additional 17 minutes and 54 seconds of overtime play. Abner Haynes, the Texans MVP running back, almost became the answer to a trivia question in that game as he won the toss and mistakenly said his team would kick the ball to the Oilers.

"I would have never lived that down, as long as I would have lived," Haynes said.

Because of extremely windy conditions, Stram wanted to force Houston to go against a strong wind. But instead of choosing to defend the proper goal, Haynes said, "We'll kick to the clock." That was the direction Stram had envisioned, but because Haynes said "We'll kick" before he gave the direction, he put his team in the hole.

That was the Texans' last game in Dallas. Hunt knew he couldn't compete with the NFL's Cowboys, so he packed the team up and headed off to Kansas City. Shortly after Hunt moved the Chiefs to the Midwest, a New York businessman named David A. "Sonny" Werblin bought the struggling Titans from the league and renamed the team the Jets.

"I believe in the star system," Werblin was often quoted as saying. "It's the only thing that sells tickets. It's what you put on the stage or the playing field that draws people."

So he went out and signed the biggest star in the football galaxy, Alabama's flamboyant quarterback, Joe Namath.

"Sonny knew what he was doing when he signed Joe," Dawson said. "He signed him to some record deal [a $427,000 contract] and everyone in New York was suddenly talking about the Jets and not the Giants."

Commissioners and team representatives of the American and National football leagues talk before the start of a House Judiciary Subcommittee hearing in Washington, D.C., on October 11, 1966. From left to right, Art Modell, president of the Cleveland Browns; Pete Rozelle, National Football League commissioner; Tex Schramm, Dallas Cowboys president; Milt Woodard, American Football League commissioner; and Lamar Hunt, president of the Kansas City Chiefs.

"When Joe walks into a room, you know he's there," Werblin said. "When another rookie walks in, he's just a nice-looking kid. Namath's like Babe Ruth or Lou Gehrig."

Namath became the face of the league, and no one was happier about that than Hunt, who saw his plan suddenly gaining some real momentum.

"Once Sonny came on board in New York, we felt a lot better about our chances," Hunt said. "He provided some real strength financially, and he also had a plan to make his team successful."

The Jets were the hottest ticket in the Big Apple, and soon the Oakland Raiders would be the talk of the West Coast. An aggressive young executive by the name of Al Davis was putting together a team that would reach the second Super Bowl. With solid and successful teams on each coast, it was time to get a new television deal.

On January 29, 1964, NBC announced a $36-million deal with the AFL to televise its games.

"That was the turning point," Hunt said. "We had some good moments before that contract was signed, and we had some rough ones after it, but that was basically the time we knew we would survive," Hunt explained. "The contract gave us some security. It gave each team about $800,000 per season and it allowed us to plan for the future. We could compete with the NFL on a more equal footing."

The NFL knew that this new league was for real, and could actually become a threat. There was talk of a merger, so NFL commissioner Pete Rozelle sent Dallas general manager Tex Schramm to talk with Hunt about a merger. Talks grew serious quickly.

While merger talks were going on, the new league replaced its commissioner with the more aggressive Davis.

"I didn't take this job with any concern about the other league," Davis said at the time. "I'm interested in winning the war and believe me, it will be a good scrap. I have the authority to do the things necessary, and we intend to be aggressive. I have been assured that all the clubs are in the mood to sign ballplayers, and that's vital. In the past, we have not operated as a league in this area."

Davis was clearly saying that the AFL would now look to sign top NFL veteran players whose contracts had expired, and that lit a fire under Rozelle and Schramm. The secret talks with Hunt escalated, and the two sides were soon able to come to terms on a merger.

On June 8, 1966, Rozelle, Hunt, and Schramm announced publicly that the two leagues had merged. The key elements to the merger agreement included:

- a combined draft, starting in 1967;
- the leagues playing a World Championship game every year;
- all existing franchises remaining at their present sites;
- interleague preseason games beginning in 1967 and a single-league schedule commencing in 1970;

- Rozelle remaining as the commissioner of the combined leagues;
- AFL clubs paying an indemnity fee of $18 million over a 20-year period;
- two franchises added by 1968, one in each league, with entry fees paid to the NFL.

The plan was approved by only a 6–3 vote of the AFL owners, but that majority was enough to push it through. As a result, the war between the two leagues came to a peaceful, productive end.

"When Tex and I talked, we were very serious," Hunt explained. "We met in Tex's car at Love Field in Dallas, and we got things done. The signing wars were costly for both leagues, and there was a desire to put it behind us before it got worse. That's why we were able to reach an agreement so quickly."

LAMAR "007" HUNT AND THE MERGER OF TWO LEAGUES

Six years after creating the American Football League, Hunt was asked about the possibility of the up-and-coming league merging with the more established NFL. It was a real cloak-and-dagger tale that Hunt loves to recall. Here is that tale of mystery in Hunt's own words.

The first meeting was right out of one of those Scotland Yard spy movies. Tex Schramm of the Dallas Cowboys and I met for the first time in a parking lot at Love Field in Dallas to talk about the possible merger of our American Football League and their NFL. I had been in Kansas City for a Chiefs function that day. Tex called me and asked if it would be possible to get together in the next few days. I was on my way to Houston from Kansas City so we agreed to meet at Love Field—at the Texas Ranger statue in the lobby at Love Field, to be exact. I said I would get off the plane and we could visit before it took off again for Houston.

I saw him at the statue, waiting, and from there we went to the parking lot and sat in his car and talked for 30 minutes in the dark. Can you imagine if there had been a security guard watching all of this—two strange men in a parked car in the airport parking lot! We wouldn't have had a chance. Anyway, that was the beginning of the merger discussions, just Tex and I at first because there were strong feelings on both sides.

Now it's 20 years since the merger and, even though I still think of it as the AFL and the NFL, it really isn't anymore. It just doesn't seem like that long because the memories are still vivid in my mind.

Over the next month, from those first days in April, Tex and I met face to face on two occasions, and there were a lot of phone conversations in between. Not too many people knew we were talking because we thought that would be best. We first started talking about how the merger might be attained, finding some common grounds of agreement just for Tex and I and then thinking about what would be accepted by others in both leagues.

We knew each other because we both lived in Dallas and we also "fought" each other in Dallas when the Texans and Cowboys were there together from 1960 through 1962. We had already fully challenged each other on the battlefield with the Dallas fans and we knew that neither of us would emerge victorious financially or in any other way, so we elected to take the AFL Texans north to Kansas City in 1963.

In 1966 there were 111 common draft choices between the two leagues. The NFL signed 79 and the AFL signed 28. Four never signed with either league.

From just a long-range standpoint, the AFL's contract with NBC-TV—a five-year agreement—was the biggest single factor in bringing the two leagues together. It was the most dramatic single

DID YOU KNOW...

Joe Montana wanted to wear either No. 3 (his number at Notre Dame) or No. 16 (his number at San Francisco) when he signed with the Chiefs, but those numbers had been retired, as they were worn by Hall of Famers Jan Stenerud (No. 3) and Len Dawson (No. 16). Montana settled on No. 19— a combination of 3 plus 16.

development. The Jets established the fact that two teams could do well in New York.

Our Texans left Dallas to the Cowboys, the Chargers left Los Angeles to the Rams and moved to San Diego, but Joe Namath and the Jets were challenging the Giants in New York and the Raiders had a big following in the Bay Area competing against the 49ers.

Yet when I look back on those times, the biggest stumbling block was the personal antagonism that had gone on for seven years between the two leagues. There was a lot of distrust. I can remember once we got our committee together—Ralph Wilson of the Bills and Billy Sullivan of the Patriots, both were original AFL owners—they were telling me that the NFL people were just leading me on. I can remember Ralph and Billy were at my home one evening and I got Tex on the phone, just so they could hear it themselves. I still have the paper with Ralph Wilson's handwriting, telling me to ask Tex certain questions as we were going through the conversation.

The negotiations almost ended when the Giants signed Pete Gogolak away from Buffalo. That started the signing war. We, that is the AFL, went after quarterbacks. Houston signed John Brodie to a future contract and there were others along the way, though Brodie's signing got the NFL's attention.

Tex and I, and probably everyone else, knew this couldn't go on. Memorial Day 1966 was the turning point. I was at the Indianapolis 500, but much of the weekend was spent on the telephone with Schramm, NFL commissioner Pete Rozelle, and our AFL committee. Tex and Pete were in Dallas.

The final terms were ironed out:

- one commissioner—Rozelle
- a championship game between the two leagues starting in '66
- interleague play beginning in the preseason of '67
- a common schedule in 1970

As I look back now, it represented an incredible struggle for survival from our standpoint. It wasn't a matter of whether the NFL was going to survive. *We* were fighting for survival. We were fighting to establish something. We had copied a successful idea.

It was a remarkable era in sports because the American Football League was the first league that had really lasted. There had been three previous American Football Leagues and they had all failed.

Although the American Football League merged into the National name and changed the name to conference, we still came as a unit and I feel proud of that because there was a lot of pride in the AFL. I think the feeling was that we had succeeded. We had kept the bill collectors away from the door long enough, the wolves away from the door, and did succeed from the standpoint of making it a viable entity.

I'm glad we merged. But I will always think of it as the AFL versus the NFL. I still keep track and always will.

ON THE VERGE OF GREATNESS

OTIS TAYLOR

Otis Taylor made the unbelievable, believable. Long before Michael Jordan or Dominique Wilkins, the Kansas City Chiefs wide receiver was a human highlight film.

"Otis made my job so easy," said quarterback Len Dawson, who made sure he always knew where his favorite wide receiver was on the playing field. "If I got it close, Otis caught it."

One of Taylor's most memorable grabs came in a game against the Washington Redskins during which he made a one-handed catch of a 28-yard touchdown pass from Dawson to seal a 27–20 victory.

"Everyone remembers that catch, and it was a great one," Dawson said, "because Pat Fischer has Otis's other hand pinned to his side, and the only way he can catch it is with one hand. But on the previous play he made an even better catch. He's on the sideline and I'm trying to throw the ball away and he reaches out and makes this great one-handed catch.

"After the game, reporters are asking me about the play and there was no way I'm going to tell them I was throwing it away. I told them I put it right where Otis could catch it. Actually, any-place you put it, he'd catch it."

Taylor made key receptions in back-to-back 1969 playoff wins over the New York Jets and the Oakland Raiders.

DID YOU KNOW...

Hank Stram was an assistant football coach at Purdue when Len Dawson was the Boilermakers' All-American quarterback.

"Otis told me the safety was guarding him and he couldn't keep up with him," Dawson said, "so we went with a deep pattern that was a bit dangerous because of the way the wind was swirling in Shea Stadium.

"I threw the ball, and for a moment I thought I'd overthrown it, but Otis had a gear other receivers didn't have and he took off and caught it. It set up a touchdown pass to Gloster Richardson and we won the game 13–6. Otis telling me about that play made the difference in the game."

The next week the Chiefs had to travel to Oakland, and again Taylor caught Dawson's ear on the sideline and suggested a play.

"Whenever we needed a big play, Otis came up with it," Dawson said. "I hit him on a 35-yard play from our 2 and that got us out of a hole. We eventually scored the go-ahead touchdown and won the game 17–7."

Taylor's most spectacular touchdown came in the Chiefs' 23–7 victory over the Minnesota Vikings in Super Bowl IV.

Dawson hit Taylor on a short swing pass and Taylor broke free along the sideline. One of the biggest and strongest wide receivers in the history of the AFL broke away from Earsell Mackbee at the 40-yard line and stiff-armed Karl Kassulke inside the 10 to complete a 46-yard touchdown that iced the victory.

"I knew the game was over right then," Dawson said. "He was such a great wide receiver, and he was a great athlete. There was no one like him back in the days of the NFL. If we had thrown the ball more to him, he would have owned every record there was."

Taylor said (back then), "I knew we needed to score because I remember the way Minnesota came back against the [Los Angeles]

Rams. I got hit, but spun away from the first guy. Then I hit the last guy with my hand. I always try to punish a defender, just like they try to punish me."

While former San Diego Chargers wide receiver Lance Alworth was the first AFL player inducted into the Hall of Fame, Taylor's Hall of Fame teammates believe he belongs in the NFL shrine.

"He's a Hall of Famer in every sense of the word," Dawson said. "He could do it all. He was a great receiver and a great blocker. We scored a lot of rushing touchdowns off Otis Taylor blocks."

Adds linebacker Bobby Bell, "Otis was the best. When we needed a big play, Otis was the man we went to. Everyone in the stadium knew what was happening, and he still made the play."

Taylor, a product of Prairie View A&M, was also a prized college recruit among NFL teams. The Dallas Cowboys wanted to sign Taylor and had him stay in a Texas hotel, where the rival AFL teams couldn't find him.

"From 1960 to 1966 was the battle over players, like when we had to sneak Otis Taylor out of the window of a motel room," Chiefs owner Lamar Hunt said. "That was 1964, the time of babysitting. Otis was a senior out of Prairie View A&M, and the Dallas Cowboys were babysitting him in a motel room to keep him away from the AFL scouts. But one of our scouts, Lloyd Welles, went into the motel and found a janitor to give a message to Otis. Otis climbed out the window of the motel, got into Lloyd's car, and was on the next flight to Kansas City. We signed him the next day."

Taylor smiles at the thought of that scenario.

"That's how it happened," said Taylor, who retired with 410 receptions for 7,306 yards and 57 touchdowns—all Chiefs records at the time.

"I am so fortunate that I got to play in Kansas City," he said. "It was a great time in my life."

MIKE GARRETT

Mike Garrett, the diminutive Heisman Trophy winner from USC, proved that good things come in small packages. He stood just

Chiefs' playmaker Mike Garrett pulls the ball to his chest after catching a pass from Len Dawson in a November 1968 game against the Boston Patriots.

5'9" and weighed 200 pounds, but as Dawson said, "He always seemed to come up with the big play."

When he signed with the Chiefs in 1966 he brought the bright lights and glamour of Southern California with him. In just five seasons he rushed for 3,246 yards and scored 24 touchdowns.

Those totals might not seem like much today, but back then the Chiefs used three different backs in a rotating tandem and Garrett made sure he made the most of every scoring opportunity.

"Coach Stram would come up with these creative game plans and you knew that every time you touched the ball, you had the chance to do something special," said Garrett, who is back at his alma mater as the university's athletics director.

Garrett scored on runs of one and 18 yards in the Chiefs AFL championship win over Buffalo and scored a big 5-yard touchdown in Super Bowl IV to secure the Chiefs win over Minnesota.

He was an All-AFL selection in 1967 when he rushed for 1,087 yards and nine touchdowns and was a member of the AFL All-Star teams in 1967 and 1968.

"He might make a 10-of-12-yard run, and run 20 or 30 yards to get the yardage," Dawson said. "He was just unstoppable in the open field and a lot of fun to watch."

CHRIS BURFORD

If Otis Taylor was a human highlight film, his wide receiver teammate Chris Burford was the opening credits. Burford, who looked like a Marine Corps recruit with his spit-and-polish crew cut, wasn't extremely fast or physical, and he couldn't jump out of a stadium.

"What made Chris so special," Dawson said, "was his hands and the way he ran a route. He could catch anything. That's because he was always in the perfect position to make a catch. You didn't have to improvise with Chris; you just threw the ball and he was right there where he was supposed to be."

The Stanford product was the master of the sideline reception, cradling a pass as he managed to keep both feet inbounds and then fall to the sideline.

"If you work hard enough at something," Burford said, "you usually got pretty good at it. And we had the best quarterback in the league in Lenny. I'm happy to know that I inspired him, because he certainly inspired me."

Dawson remembers one pass play in which two defenders were between him and Burford, but he says, "I still threw the ball. I just knew he was going to catch it."

And he did.

When Burford retired in 1967 he was the team's all-time leading receivers with 391 receptions for 5,505 yards and 55 touchdowns.

"We spent a lot of time after practice working on routes," Dawson said, "and it all paid off. You would see him make a catch and the defensive back would just shake his head in disgust."

FRED ARBANAS

To play tight end in the AFL, you have to have the speed and power of a fullback, the hands of a wide receiver, and the strength and power of a guard or tackle. As the All-Time AFL tight end, Fred Arbanas had those attributes and more.

The Michigan State grad starred on two Super Bowl teams, and though he doesn't have the gaudy numbers of players who play that position today, he retired with 198 receptions and 3,101 yards—which were Chiefs records until Tony Gonzalez came along.

"Fred was a man's man," Dawson said. "He was the guy who brought his lunch box to work, punched the time clock, and gave it everything he had every down."

AFL through and through, when the Chiefs hammered the Chicago Bears 66–24 in an exhibition game following their loss to the Green Bay Packers in the first Super Bowl, owner Lamar Hunt heard Arbanas say, "That's the one win I will always remember."

A more memorable win came in Super Bowl IV, when Arbanas's blocking played a key role in a 23–7 win over Minnesota.

While Arbanas was a part of many great victories, his greatest might have been overcoming the loss of sight in his left eye following an attack in downtown Kansas City.

"I was lying in a hospital bed convinced my football career was over," said Arbanas, a six-time All-AFL tight end. "I left the hospital and went to practice and my eye started to hemorrhage. I had to have an operation and lost the sight in that eye, and I thought my football career was over."

Little did Arbanas know that Stram placed a patch over his left eye and had his sons toss him a football as he ran Arbanas's routes in his back yard.

"I wanted to see if Freddy could still see the ball," Stram explained. "When I did that, I realized he could still see the ball and I was going to give him every opportunity to come back to the team," sais Arbanas.

While he recovered, Arbanas played catch with his own son, and he too found out he could follow the flight of the ball with just one eye.

"I met Hank and Lenny at our training facility and Hank told me he knew I could play again. And after a while, I began to believe him."

After hours of extra sessions with Dawson, Arbanas regained his confidence and enjoyed six more years in the league.

Today he is a Jackson County legislator and has a golf course named after him in Lee's Summit, Missouri.

JERRY MAYS

There have been hundreds of captains in the history of the Kansas City Chiefs, but there will only be one "Captain."

"The Captain?" asked Hall of Fame linebacker Bell. "That's Jerry Mays."

Mays was the glue that kept the Chiefs defensive line together during the glory years in both Dallas and Kansas City. He stood just 6'4" and weighed in at 240 pounds, but he often said, "You can't measure a man's heart."

And the former cocaptain at Southern Methodist University was right.

"Jerry was the only man I ever coached," Stram said, "who could play at an all-star level at every position on the line."

Jerry Mays was a team captain and anchor on the Chiefs' defensive line and represented the spirit of the AFL perhaps more than anyone else in the league. Photo courtesy of Bettmann/Corbis.

Mays was named to the All-Time AFL All-Star team and was All-AFL as a defensive tackle two times and as an end four times.

"I was an old-fashioned player," Mays told Dick Connor. "I was one of Hank's boys. I believed in everything he did. It got a little corny at times, but I just loved everything about it."

And more than any of the Chiefs, Mays was AFL through and through.

"I loved the AFL," said Mays, who retired in 1970 following the win in Super Bowl IV.

"It was part of me and the merger with the NFL made it easier to retire. I know it was a business decision, but it took a lot of fun out of it. I was AFL from start to finish, proud of the league, tickled to death I'd played in it. It was always the little guy against the big guy and I liked that."

While he didn't overpower many opponents, Mays used his agility and quick feet to throw a stunned running back for a loss or sack a quarterback at a key moment in the game.

"He just loved to play," Dawson said. "I think Jerry Mays would have played for free."

Mays was a successful businessman in Texas when he lost a long battle with cancer in 1994.

JERREL WILSON

Say the word *Thunderfoot* and watch a grin come to the face of any member of the Kansas City Chiefs who played with Jerrel Wilson.

He is another member of the team whose AFL exploits should land him in the Football Hall of Fame because, as Coach Stram once said, "You can't compare any other punter to Jerrel Wilson. That wouldn't be fair."

When the Chiefs were in trouble, they would call on "Thunderfoot" to bail them out.

"He was amazing," Dawson said. "He was just so powerful. He did things you just don't see anymore."

Wilson starred for the Chiefs for 15 seasons and was named the All-Time All-AFL punter. He owns team records for the most punts (1,018), average yards per punt in a career (43.4), a season (46.1), and a game (56.4). He had four career punts over 70 yards and was named to three Pro Bowl teams following the merger in 1970.

Wilson passed away in 2005.

EMMITT THOMAS

Emmitt Thomas wasn't a glitzy number one draft pick when he signed with the Chiefs in 1966.

He wasn't even a draft pick. He came to Kansas City as a free agent out of tiny Bishop College in Dallas and starred in the secondary for 13 years, with 58 career interceptions, a team record.

"We knew about Emmitt and were excited to sign him," Stram said, "but we never anticipated him making such an impact on the team."

This 6'2", 192-pound diamond in the rough quickly proved he belonged in the league as he led the AFL with nine interceptions and always seemed to select the biggest stage to enjoy a great game.

"I remember Emmitt picking off a pass in Super Bowl IV," Dawson said. "He was just an extremely smart player and very gifted. He was strong and fast and became the prototype for the secondary."

From 1966 to 1978 he anchored a secondary that was second to none. When he left the Chiefs, he joined the NFL coaching ranks. He has been the secondary coach for the Atlanta Falcons the past six years.

ED BUDDE

Here's an interesting trivia question: who was the first member of the Kansas City Chiefs offensive line to be named the AFL's Offensive Player of the Week?

The answer is guard Ed Budde.

His performance in a 24–10 win against Oakland back in 1968 made him the first interior lineman to ever win the award in the history of the AFL. In that game, Coach Stram threw an old T-formation offense at the Raiders and the Chiefs gained 215 yards on the ground in the first half alone. Budde and tackle Jim Tyrer were credited with blocking on 111 of those yards. "I've never seen a guard play like that," right tackle Dave Hill said in *The Kansas City Star*. "It was the best game an offensive lineman can have."

Added tight end Arbanas, "No guard can play like that."

No one appreciated Budde's performance more than quarterback Dawson.

"Ed was amazing," Dawson said. "He's another guy who should be in the Hall of Fame. He was just the best. And he was the best for 14 years."

Budde starred for the Chiefs for 14 years—an amazing feat when one considers the punishment an offensive lineman receives on every play.

The Michigan State product was the Chiefs' number one draft pick in 1963 and is another member of the Chiefs on the All-Time

AFL team. He appeared in five AFL All-Star Games and two NFL Pro Bowl games and started on two Super Bowl teams.

He stood 6'5" and weighed 260 pounds and dominated his position like no other player during his era. One of his greatest thrills though came after he retired. The Chiefs drafted his son Brad out of USC, and he played for the Chiefs from 1980 to 1986.

Budde works for a beer distributorship in Kansas City.

E.J. HOLUB

With his Texas twang, his 10-gallon cowboy hat, and a walk that made him look like he just got off a bucking bronco, former Chiefs linebacker and center E.J. Holub was one of a kind.

"You just hear the mention of his name and you smile," Dawson said. "He was a fiery competitor who loved the game. You know, he's the only guy to start two Super Bowls at two different positions."

Dawson is correct, as Holub was a starting linebacker in the first Super Bowl and was Dawson's center in Super Bowl IV.

E.J. Holub was another Chiefs throwback who played hurt and always played with unmatched enthusiasm. Photo courtesy of Getty Images.

During his 10-year career he had nine knee operations.

"I look like I lost a knife fight with a midget," Holub said as he gently placed a wad of chewing tobacco into his mouth. "But dad-gummit, it was worth every minute of it."

Those operations have taken a toll on the likeable Texan, who has had a total of 18 surgeries and today has an artificial hip that allows him to ride the ponies on his Oklahoma ranch and get in the occasional round of golf.

Holub was a five-time AFL All-Star linebacker who had to change positions after he tore his hamstring in 1967.

"I didn't have any mobility after I tore my hamstring," he said. "Heck, I could put up with the knee operations. Drain a little fluid off before the game and I was ready to go. But that hamstring was a different kind of injury. But I didn't let it keep me from playing."

Holub was known as the "Holler Guy" because he was always on the sideline encouraging his teammates.

"No one gave more to the game than E.J.," Dawson said. "You'd see him in the training room and think there's no way he could play and he comes out and has a great game. I think that's why the fans always loved him so much."

Holub is a throwback to the days when the game was played on real grass and the men who performed in the trenches were a special breed.

"I think the game has changed," he said. "I'm glad I played when I did. I think we were closer and cared more about each other. Today, a lot of it seems like a business. To us, it was a game."

It was a game he dominated and loved.

JIM TYRER

Jim Tyrer was known as the big man with the big heart.

"When they made Jim Tyrer," coach Hank Stram said, "they broke the mold. He was the tackle you judged every other tackle against. He was the best."

Another member of the All-Time AFL team, Tyrer was selected to nine All-Star teams for the AFL and NFL and started an amazing

180 consecutive games, never missing the call to battle during his 13-year career.

"He made it look easy," said Chiefs running back Mike Garrett, the beneficiary of countless Tyrer blocks. "He would take on two blockers and this huge hole."

Tyrer threw the block that sprung Garrett for a touchdown in Super Bowl IV.

"With the amount of strain during that game, it took me nearly a week to sit down and realize what we had accomplished," Tyrer told Dick Connor. "There was so much leading up to that game. I think the big plus was that we had been there before. There was great pressure playing for our league against the NFL."

Tyrer, who stood 6'6" and weighed 270 pounds, credits Stram for teaching him about the game he dominated.

"Coach Stram was a stickler for details," he said. "He expects a consistent attitude, eliminating peaks and valleys on good Sundays and bad Sundays. Hank puts everything in one word: *Win*."

Len Dawson believes Tyrer and Budde should both be in the Hall of Fame.

"Jim was just massive," Dawson said. "There were never two better offensive linemen on the same team than Jim and Ed [Budde]. I just don't understand why they aren't in the Hall of Fame."

Tyrer died in 1980.

JIM LYNCH

When you play alongside two of the best linebackers in the modern era, it's easy to get overlooked. That's what happened to Notre Dame graduate Jim Lynch, who played 11 years for the Chiefs and retired the same day as his Hall of Fame teammate and friend, Willie Lanier.

"Jim was a great, great linebacker," said Lanier, who followed Bell into the Hall of Fame to become just the second Chiefs player to gain such an honor. "He was overlooked, and that's a shame because he could do it all."

But Lynch has no complaints.

"It's just an honor to be mentioned in the same breath with Bobby Bell and Willie Lanier," said Lynch, the cocaptain of Notre Dame's 1966 national championship team. "I played with two of the best linebackers in the history of the game for eight seasons [1967–74] and have many great memories."

While he is not a member of the Pro Football Hall of Fame, Lynch was inducted into the College Football Hall of Fame in 1992.

JOHNNY ROBINSON

For 12 years Johnny Robinson was a master thief. However, he didn't prey on unsuspecting victims or work his special magic on a safe located behind a painting in the master bedroom of a corporate executive. He conducted his brand of thievery in front of thousands of fans on Sunday afternoons from October through December as he anchored one of the best secondaries in the AFL and NFL for more than a decade.

He led the team in interceptions from his safety position and finished with 57 career thefts, sixth in NFL history at the time (he was third all time in the AFL), and he is a member of the All-Time All-AFL team.

"When we needed a big interception to turn the game around, we looked to Johnny," Dawson said. "He just had a knack for making big plays."

Robinson was Dawson's roommate the week before Super Bowl IV, and the Hall of Fame quarterback recalls a conversation about the game.

"The Vikings were heavily favored, and I asked Johnny if he thought we could beat them, and he said, 'Heck yes.' That was good enough for me."

The Chiefs claimed a 23–7 victory and Robinson extinguished any last-gasp attempt by the Vikings to make a late comeback. As he sat on the ground clutching the ball, Robinson thrust his fist and index finger into the air to signify that the Chiefs were number one.

While he was a star in the AFL and NFL, Robinson went on to enjoy a much greater calling when he retired in 1971. The former member of the 1959 LSU national championship football team opened his sprawling Monroe, Louisiana, home to troubled youths—many of whom simply call him "Dad." Perhaps he felt a bit guilty after making life miserable for so many quarterbacks over the years that he wanted to give something back to the youth of his native Louisiana.

DERON CHERRY

Deron Cherry, free-agent punter.

Huh?

Well, how about Deron Cherry, six-time Pro Bowl free safety and the preeminent NFL defensive back of the 1980s?

That sounds more like it.

Cherry, one of the most popular players in the history of the Chiefs, came from the type of humble beginnings one often associates with afternoon children's specials or dime novels from the 1950s.

Cherry wasn't sure if he could make it in the NFL when his former defensive coach at Rutgers, Ted Cottrell, joined the staff of Chiefs coach Marv Levy.

"Ted called me and asked if I had ever signed with anyone," Cherry said. "I told him Cleveland was getting ready to offer me a contract and he told me to get on a plane and come to Kansas City before I signed anything."

Cherry tried out as a punter but didn't make the final cut. When he turned his playbook in to Levy, he reminded the coach that he played in the Rutgers secondary.

"I was disappointed when I was cut," Cherry said, "but I knew I could play in the NFL."

Opportunity knocked for Cherry when veteran strong safety Herb Christopher was injured in the first game of the 1981 season and the Chiefs called Cherry. Several players were placed on injured reserve and the Chiefs signed Cherry to back up All-Pro free safety Gary Green.

"I was part of a secondary that included Gary Green, Gary Barbaro, and Eric Harris," Cherry said. "I was playing with the best players of their time."

Barbaro soon signed a free-agent contract to play in the USFL and Cherry was now the starting safety on one of the game's top defensive units.

"I know there were skeptics," he said, "but I had faith in my ability. I never wanted to just make the roster. I wanted to start and be considered one of the best players on the team."

One of Cherry's finest moments came during the 1985 season, when he thrilled a standing-room-only crowd at Arrowhead Stadium by picking off Seattle's Dave Krieg four times in a 28–7 victory. The four interceptions tied the NFL single-game high.

"The one thing I remember about that game," Cherry said, "was catching the four balls. But I also remember not catching a ball the five other times I had a chance for an interception."

Another memorable moment for Cherry came in 1990, when he battled back from a severe knee injury to rejoin his teammates in a game against the Los Angeles Raiders.

"There were times I thought about giving up," Cherry said, "because the pain was unbearable. It brought tears to my eyes. I kept asking myself, 'Is it worth it?' And I kept answering, 'Yes.'"

The hard work paid off in a 9–7 victory over the Raiders when he made a jarring tackle on Bo Jackson and knocked the ball loose. It was recovered by Albert Lewis, and Nick Lowery followed with a field goal.

Teammate Derrick Thomas said at the time, "The man let that play make his statement. Deron Cherry is back."

When he retired in 1991, Cherry was third on the Chiefs all-time list for interceptions (50) and led the team in tackles four times and in interceptions six times.

He still resides in Kansas City, where he is a successful businessman and philanthropist.

NICK LOWERY

Nick Lowery's introduction to the NFL was a humbling experience. The Kansas City Chiefs all-time scoring leader (1,466) will forever be known as the man who replaced Hall of Fame legend Jan Stenerud. But Lowery's introduction to Kansas City came after 11 failed attempts with other teams.

"After I was cut by the New York Jets for the second time, I told myself that I was going to give it one more shot in Kansas City," Lowery said. "At the time, I was able to see that being cut had its healthy side. It prepared me incrementally for the life of a professional football player."

When Coach Levy decided to go with a younger kicker, he handed Stenerud his walking papers and began an association with Lowery and the Chiefs that lasted 14 remarkable seasons. While known to most football fans as one of the most accurate place-kickers in the game, Lowery was much more than a jock. He worked for President Reagan in Drug Abuse Policy, and for both President Bush and President Clinton in the White House Office of National Service.

His Adult Role Models for Youth (ARMY) program (now known as Youthfriends) used high-profile mentors such as professional athletes to engage more citizens in regular mentoring relationships with inner-city youth in Kansas City, and was recognized by the International YMCA in 1992. Youthfriends now connects Kansas City's youth-serving agencies with its school districts, and serves 13,000 young people with 3,000 volunteers in the Kansas City metro area.

Lowery set all-time NFL records for accuracy and field goals, was chosen for seven All-NFL teams, and kicked the game-winning points in three NFL Pro Bowls and 15 NFL games.

A graduate of Dartmouth College, Lowery is also the first pro athlete to graduate with a masters from the Harvard Kennedy School of Government.

In 1993–94, Lowery helped launch Americorps, which brought a domestic Peace Corps challenge to America's communities. In 1995 he was approached by Johns Hopkins Center for

American Indian Health to apply his urban-youth ARMY programs to teachings to Native American youth and families. Native Vision is a sports and life skills program that has reached thousands of American Indian youth from over 30 tribes with the help of the NFL Players Association for the past eight years. Native Vision and Nation Building for Native Youth, which was also founded by Lowery, are nationally recognized leadership programs. Lowery is also vice chair of the prestigious new National Fund for Excellence in American Indian Education.

"Today," Lowery writes on his website (www.nicklowery.com), "athletes have a remarkable spotlight on them. We can encourage, enlighten, and empower people to ask better questions, solve their own problems, and tell their own stories of triumph."

If ever there was a story of triumph, it is Lowery's story of accomplishment on and off the playing field.

NEIL SMITH

Neil Smith was known as a big man with an even bigger heart. The latest addition to the Kansas City Chiefs Arrowhead Stadium Ring of Fame, the former number one draft pick out of Nebraska made quite a name for himself in the NFL. He was a member of the NFL's 75th Anniversary team and teamed with linebacker Thomas to form one of the most feared pass rushing duos of the 1990s.

The defense that was anchored by Thomas and Smith was a big reason the Chiefs reached postseason play for six straight years (1990–95). He left Kansas City in 1996 and went on to win two Super Bowl rings with the Denver Broncos. His Kansas City totals in sacks (86.5) and forced fumbles (29) rank second only to Thomas's.

"I was a number one draft pick in 1988 and I got off to a rough start," said Smith, who was considered a disappointment until Marty Schottenheimer came along in 1989 and began working with the budding superstar. "When Derrick got drafted number one in 1989, I kind of took him under my wing. I called him my

Chiefs defensive end Neil Smith sets his sights on Colts quarterback Jim Harbaugh during an AFC playoff game in January 1996.

little buddy and we looked out for each other. We had a lot of fun and experienced a lot of ups and downs, but I loved my time in Kansas City.

"My only regret is that I couldn't help bring the Super Bowl trophy back to Kansas City and Mr. [Lamar] Hunt. When I first stepped foot on to this field, that was my first goal. We never got that done, but we still have some great memories to savor."

PRIEST HOLMES

A new marshal arrived in the NFL in 1998, and his name wasn't Faulk. It was Priest Holmes, a running back who let his actions on the field do most of his talking. While former St. Louis Rams star Marshall Faulk was breaking all kinds of rushing records, Holmes was trying to break into the Kansas City Chiefs' starting lineup.

Once he did, he was unstoppable. He led the NFL in rushing in 2001 with 1,555 yards and followed that campaign with 1,615 yards in just 14 games. Just when it appeared he would break Faulk's single-season touchdown mark of 26, he injured his hip in the 15th game of the season and had to settle for a league-high 24 scores.

While many so-called experts said the quiet young man from Texas would never rebound from the hip injury he suffered in Denver, he proved them all wrong. Holmes enjoyed one of the finest seasons in the history of the NFL in 2003 when he rushed for 1,420 yards and scored a then–NFL record 27 touchdowns.

"When you tell Priest he can't do something," former teammate Tony Richardson said, "he's going to prove you wrong. When everyone was saying he won't be back, I knew he'd be back and I knew he'd be better than ever."

Injuries have limited Priest Holmes potential legacy, but he was the game's most dangerous runner for a period.

Injuries still continue to haunt Holmes, who was unable to play in 2006 because of a neck injury he suffered in the eighth game of the 2005 season. While he hasn't formally retired, it appears as though this Priest has performed his miracles for the Chiefs and is content to pass the torch to Larry Johnson.

IT AIN'T OVER 'TIL IT'S OVER

A DAY THE DEFENSE RULED

One yard of torn up, battered turf was all that stood between the New York Jets and a return to the AFL Championship Game. The Jets had stunned the world in 1969 by beating the Baltimore Colts in Super Bowl III, and Joe Namath and Company looked to be ready to return to the big game as they faced the Kansas City Chiefs.

The wind was howling and swirling at Shea Stadium as Namath marched his team to the Chiefs' 1-yard line. The Chiefs were clinging to a 6–3 lead late in the fourth quarter. They knew that if they allowed a touchdown, it would be tough to get back into the game because of the wind that whipped across the field. It was so ferocious that Kansas City punter Jerrel Wilson whiffed on a practice attempt on the sideline as the ball blew onto the playing field.

"Our defensive stand in that game," Chiefs Hall of Fame linebacker Willie Lanier said, "was inspirational. It was the most significant single defense series I was ever a part of."

Chiefs defensive lineman Jerry Mays said at the time, "It was something that doesn't happen in 10 or 20 years. We were high. It was indescribable. The defensive unit had played well the entire game; then Willie got us. He fired me up. It was the way he did it—tears in his eyes, teeth gnashing."

Defending Super Bowl champion quarterback Joe Namath of the New York Jets leaves the field in a cloud of dust after the Chiefs' famous defensive stand sealed their playoff victory at Shea Stadium in New York.

Bill Mathis got the first carry and was stopped for no gain. Matt Snell, the Super Bowl hero from the year before, then lost half a yard. Namath knew the run wasn't going to work, so he faked a pitchout to Snell, turned, and faked a handoff to Mathis, then looked for Snell in the flat.

By instinct, Hall of Fame linebacker Bobby Bell was standing there, preventing Namath from throwing the pass. To avoid a sack, Namath threw the ball at Snell's feet and the Jets had to settle for a Jim Turner field goal.

"Bell had no business being there," Namath said.

While the defense was keeping the Jets in check, Chiefs wide receiver Otis Taylor approached Len Dawson about a possible pass play.

"There were times our receivers would come up to me on the sideline and talk about a possible play," Dawson said. "Otis knelt down on the sideline and actually diagramed this play in the turf.

"He said the free safety can't guard me and he came up with this play and I thought to myself, 'That can work.' As we went out to the field on our next series, Otis came up to me and said, 'Think you'll call the play?' Well, with my sense of humor, I replied, 'No, not until we get in the huddle.'

"The play Otis came up with worked to perfection. Now, you have to understand that the wind was blowing and it was cold and miserable and Joe was having a hard time getting his passes to do what he wanted them to do. A lot of the passes he was throwing were just dying out there, getting knocked down by the wind.

"I knew I needed a good release and a good spiral and I let the ball go. At first I thought I'd thrown it too far, but thank goodness Otis has a different gear and he catches up with the ball and it goes for about a 61-yard gain."

The Chiefs had the ball on the Jets' 19-yard line and Dawson hit Gloster Richardson for the game-winning touchdown pass on the next play. Namath marched the Jets to the Chiefs 16- and 13-yard lines later in the quarter, but could not find the end zone.

"I'll never forget that game as long as I live," Bell said. "I don't think a defense can play any better than we played that day."

REVENGE IS SWEET FOR CHIEFS

There was certainly no love lost between the competitors in the 1969 AFL Championship Game.

"We hated the Raiders and they hated us," Hall of Fame linebacker Bobby Bell said. "They had our number back then, and we knew we had to play a perfect game to get a win and go on to the Super Bowl."

The Raiders had defeated the Chiefs twice during the regular season.

Following their 13–6 victory over the Jets, the Chiefs traveled to sunny California to take on the Raiders. In an ironic twist, they stayed at the same hotel the Green Bay Packers had occupied when they beat the Chiefs in the first Super Bowl. Hank Stram even stayed in Vince Lombardi's suite.

Stram wanted to wipe aside the memory of recent Raiders victories and stressed that the only game that counted "was the next one." The Chiefs practiced in black and silver jerseys because Stram wanted his players to visually recognize their Raider counterparts.

Because the Super Bowl was going to be played in New Orleans, the Raiders staged a luncheon before the game with a Mardi Gras theme. When the Chiefs heard about it, they were furious.

"Hank was really mad," Bell said, "and it fired the rest of us up. Not that we really needed to be fired up to play the Raiders."

The Raiders did everything right in a first quarter that saw them take a quick 7–0 lead. They totaled 101 yards and hit pay dirt on a three-yard run by Charlie Smith. The Chiefs defense stiffened, but the offense didn't get a first down until midway through the second quarter.

"Although the Raiders had dominated us for the past three seasons and the first half of that game," Dawson said, "there was no panic on our part. We trailed 7–0 but felt like something good was going to happen."

With just under three minutes to play until the half, the Chiefs offense began to click. Dawson hit Taylor for a 13-yard play. A couple of Raiders penalties and a run by Robert Holmes pushed the ball into Oakland territory.

Dawson hit Frank Pitts in stride as he raced down the sideline, and only a touchdown-saving tackle by Nemiah Wilson on the 1-yard line kept the speedy receiver from scoring. It didn't matter as fullback Wendell Hayes scored on the next play, and it was knotted 7–7 at the half.

Aaron Brown, the Chiefs' massive young defensive lineman, turned the game around at the start of the third quarter when he rushed quarterback Daryle Lamonica, who hit his hand on

Kansas City's Robert Holmes slips into the corner of the end zone past Raiders linebacker Chip Oliver for the go-ahead touchdown in the 1969 AFL Championship Game. Photo courtesy of Bettmann/Corbis.

Brown's helmet as he attempted a pass play. It was apparent Lamonica had hurt his hand as he bobbled a snap on a 39-yard field goal attempt by George Blanda.

The Chiefs couldn't capitalize on their good fortune, however, as Mike Garrett fumbled the ball on the next series, but once again Brown came at Lamonica and forced an incomplete pass. His hand too tender to play, Lamonica turned quarterbacking duties over to the legendary Blanda, who drove the Raiders deep into Chiefs territory. With the ball on the Kansas City 24-yard line, Blanda saw Warren Wells alone near the 5-yard line. He threw a perfect pass, but Wells slipped and the ball was intercepted by Emmitt Thomas in the end zone. Smith returned the ball to the 6, and Dawson and his offense went to work. Holmes was tackled for a four-yard loss and Dawson looked to his big play man to get the team out of this hole.

"We had a play where Otis Taylor lined up between the guard and tackle and took off toward the sideline," Dawson said. "I called Otis's number and threw the ball so only he could catch it—which he did."

The Chiefs had a first down on their own 37-yard line. Holmes ran for six, caught a 23-yard pass, and then Wilson was called for interference against Taylor on the 7-yard line.

Two plays later Holmes scored from the 5-yard line and the Chiefs had a 14–7 lead.

"The way our defense was playing," Dawson said, "we felt pretty confident. But we wanted to put more points on the scoreboard."

The Chiefs fumbled the ball away three times in the fourth quarter, but the defense managed to hold the Raiders in check and set up the final score of the afternoon. Lamonica returned to the game and was intercepted by Thomas, who returned the pick 62 yards. That set up a 22-yard Jan Stenerud field goal. Brown was credited with three sacks in the game and Blanda and Lamonica combined for 17 of 45 completions for just 154 yards.

"In back-to-back weeks, our defense held Joe Namath and the Jets to two field goals and the Raiders to one touchdown," Dawson said. "I think that is too often overlooked."

As the Chiefs boarded their bus to make the trip to the airport, Stram called to Bell, who had just left the locker room.

"Coach pointed over to some Raiders," Bell said. "They were carrying their suitcases home. They thought they were going to New Orleans. But all they were doing was going home."

COMING THROUGH IN THE CLUTCH

GAMBLING PROBE NO DISTRACTION FOR SUPER BOWL IV MVP DAWSON

The one thing any player wants to avoid before the biggest moment of his life, his once chance to stand center stage with the spotlight in his face, is an unnecessary distraction.

"You've got that right," chuckled Len Dawson, the Kansas City Chiefs Hall of Fame quarterback and the MVP of Super Bowl IV.

"You especially want to avoid the type of distractions that come from the nightly news."

As Dawson and his teammates prepared for the Super Bowl, it was reported on a national newscast that Dawson was one of several players who would have to testify before a grand jury in Detroit that was looking into a gambling investigation.

"Now I've been blindsided in my day, but never like that," said Dawson, who professed his innocence. "And I wasn't the only one named—they named Joe [Namath] and some other current and former quarterbacks and Bob Devaney [the legendary head football coach] at Nebraska. We were supposed to get subpoenas in 10 days."

Ten days came and went and no subpoena arrived.

"Never did get one," Dawson said, shaking his head. "Today, all the talk is about steroids and cheating in sports. Back then, if your name was associated with gambling, that was like the kiss of death."

In the midst of an unsubstantiated gambling probe, Len Dawson (No. 16) and teammates rallied together to defeat the Vikings in Super Bowl IV. Photo courtesy of Getty Images.

Gambling problems have kept Pete Rose, baseball's all-time hits leader, out of the Hall of Fame. Former NFL commissioner Pete Rozelle suspended former greats Alex Karras and Hall of Famer Paul Hornung for gambling.

Now Dawson was in the eye of the hurricane. Police officers found his name in the phone directory of Donald Dawson (no relation), a known gambler who had over $400,000 in checks and cashier's checks in his possession at the time of his arrest.

"He had my number and a lot of players' numbers," Dawson said. "I'd met him when I played for Pittsburgh. That was 10 years ago. When I hurt my knee [during the 1969 season that led up to Super Bowl IV], he called me. When my father passed away that same season, he called again. That was it. Now, this big investigation is going on and everyone is asking me what I want to do."

Dawson's answer was simple.

"Tell them the truth," he said. "I knew the guy. I wasn't going to make matters worse by saying I didn't know him."

Because of the intense media scrutiny, Dawson left his room in the Fountainbleau Hotel and moved into head coach Hank Stram's suite.

"I don't think Johnny [Robinson, Dawson's roommate] has ever forgotten me," Dawson said, grinning. "He got calls around the clock—and they were all for me."

Dawson met with team owner Lamar Hunt, Stram, and team officials and devised a plan. He then gave the following statement (reprinted courtesy of the Kansas City Chiefs):

> "My name has been mentioned in regard to an investigation conducted by the Justice Department. I have not been contacted by any law enforcement agency or apprised of any reason why my name has been brought up. The only reason I can think of is that I have a casual acquaintance with Mr. Donald Dawson of Detroit, who I understand has been charged in the investigation. Mr. Dawson is not a relative of mine. I have known Mr. Dawson for about 10 years and have talked with him on several occasions. My only conversations with him in recent years concerned my knee injury and the death of my father. On these occasions he called me to offer his sympathy. These calls were among the many I received. Gentlemen, this is all I have to say. I have told you everything I know."

The next morning Dawson read the same statement in front of his teammates. When he was done, Stram asked if there were any questions.

"Yeah, have our tickets come in yet?" asked center E.J. Holub.

Like his teammates, Holub knew that Dawson was innocent and he was steamed that his friend and the team had to face such allegations.

"It made us mad," linebacker Bobby Bell said, "and fired us up. I think it might have helped us come together as a team."

Because he was forthright and addressed the issue head on, the media scrutiny soon subsided for Dawson—but not his family.

"My family really had it tough," Dawson said. "I was getting ready for the Super Bowl, my kids were in school, and kids were asking them if their dad was a gambler, and my wife had to answer questions at the grocery store. That's the part that still makes me mad. They shouldn't have been a part of it. I'm a big boy and I can handle a situation like that, but they should have been left out of it."

In retrospect, Dawson believes Rozelle wanted to confront him about the allegations before the Chiefs defeated the Oakland Raiders in the AFL Championship Game in Oakland.

"The night before the [AFL Championship] game, I got a call in my hotel room from Pete Rozelle," Dawson said. "I was wondering why the commissioner was calling me. He probably wanted to talk to me about it, but all he did was wish me luck. I thought that was strange."

Dawson, who ironically went on to broadcast NFL games on NBC, still wonders why the network decided to run the story just a few days before the Super Bowl.

"The game was big back then," he said, "but nothing like it is today. If Peyton Manning was involved in something like that and read a statement to the media, it would be broadcast all over the world. I mean, it would be broadcast in China, for goodness sake. NBC was televising the AFL Championship Game and CBS had the rights to the Super Bowl. Some people think that NBC was trying to steal the thunder away from the Super Bowl, but we'll never know, will we?"

To make matters worse for Dawson, he became ill the night before the game and could only manage to eat a few crackers, a candy bar, and drink some milk. Over the past year, Dawson had suffered a knee injury that sidelined him for five games and he lost his father, who died before the playoff game against the New York Jets. Now he was about to face the challenge of going against the Purple People Eaters from Minnesota, who were chomping at the bit to reclaim the NFL's honor after the AFL's upstart Jets had claimed an upset win over Baltimore in Super Bowl III.

A REAL SWINGER

As George Brett approached the vaunted 3,000-hit mark in his Hall of Fame baseball career, Kansas City Chiefs defensive lineman Neil Smith wanted to pay a special tribute to the Kansas City Royals third baseman/designated hitter.

"I'm a big baseball fan, a big George Brett fan," said Smith, the number two all-time sack leader in Chiefs history. "So when George got close to 3,000, I wanted to do something special."

He thought about it for a while and finally decided on taking a lofty swing, as though he was swinging a baseball bat, following each sack.

If Smith was playing at Arrowhead Stadium, he would point to the section where Brett and his family have their season tickets and then take the mighty hack.

"When I found out Neil was doing that in honor of me, I thought it was pretty cool," said Brett, a longtime Chiefs season ticket holder. "When a guy like Neil Smith, who is going to be in the Pro Football Hall of Fame someday, pays you a tribute, it's really special."

Dawson started out throwing smart, short passes that led to a then–Super Bowl record 48-yard field goal by Jan Stenerud. Dawson was methodical, slicing up the Vikings like a surgeon, taking what the defense gave him and making the most of every running back and wide receiver on the team. The Chiefs took a 9–0 lead into the half as Stenerud kicked three field goals.

"The first field goal meant a lot," Stenerud said. "The second [from 32 yards] didn't mean as much, but the third [from 25 yards] was big because it meant they couldn't tie the game with a touchdown."

Before the half Dawson moved the team to the 5-yard line, where Mike Garrett scored a touchdown that sent the Chiefs into the locker room with a 16–0 lead.

Dawson maintained his composure during the halftime break, thinking to himself, "The way our defense is playing today, we can win this thing with one more touchdown."

Minnesota finally got on the scoreboard in the third quarter when Dave Osborn scored on a four-yard run, but the Chiefs roared back and put the game out of Minnesota's reach on one of the most memorable pass plays in Kansas City history. It was a pass from Dawson to Taylor in the right flat.

"There wasn't much to the pass," Dawson said. "Otis did all the work."

Taylor, using long strides as he raced down the sideline, sidestepped Earsell Mackbee, then stiff-armed Karl Kassulke near the 10-yard line to make the score 23–7.

The touchdown set off a wild celebration on the Chiefs sideline as they had finally exorcised the demons that came from losing the first Super Bowl.

"It was just a great feeling to be in a winning locker room," said Dawson, who received a congratulatory phone call from President Nixon after the game. "That was the last time an AFL team would ever play an NFL team, because of the merger, and we came out on top."

THE NIGERIAN NIGHTMARE

As a youngster growing up in Enugu, Nigeria, Christian Okoye recalls the horrors of a civil conflict that tore his country apart.

"I would be standing on a corner and see men coming at me with machine guns," the former Kansas City Chiefs Pro Bowl running back said. "I would wake up at night and hear gun shots or walk down the street and hide in an alley, fearful that I might be shot and killed. It was a very bad time."

No wonder the man who earned the nickname "the Nigerian Nightmare" never seemed to be intimidated by opposing defensive players.

"When you went through what I went through," he said, with a warm and gentle smile, "nothing would scare you. Football was a game. It wasn't war, it was a game."

When Okoye was six, Ibo insurgents seceded from Nigeria and created the Republic of Biafra. War ravaged Okoye's homeland from

1967 to 1970, and he wondered if he might ever sleep through the night, "without being awakened by the sound of gunfire."

A deeply religious man, Okoye grew up to become Africa's top discus (212 feet, two inches), hammer throw (219 feet, seven inches), and shot put (59 feet, two inches) champion.

"I came to the United States to compete in track," Okoye said. "I didn't know what football was until I came to the United States."

That was back in 1982, when he attended tiny Azusa Pacific College in southeast California. He was a seven-time NAIA track champion in four different events, but when he was denied the opportunity to compete in the 1984 Olympics by a group of Nigerian track officials, he decided to try football.

"That was the best choice of my life," Okoye said. "I was so sad when I couldn't compete in the Olympics, and Coach [Jim] Milhon had talked to me about playing football. To me, football meant soccer. I had no idea what it was. I didn't even know how to put on the shoulder pads."

But he was a quick study. After rushing for minus one yard on two carries in his college debut, he rushed for more than 100 yards in 16 of his next 18 games. His 4.38 speed caught the attention of pro scouts. When he scored four touchdowns in the Senior Bowl, everyone began to take notice.

"When I saw him on film, my hands began to sweat—he was that exciting," said former Kansas City Chiefs head coach Frank Gansz. "He was explosive because of his track training. He was bigger than most of the linemen he played against in college. We just had to teach him the game."

After one intense practice session, his former offensive lineman teammate cried out, "Watch out! Here comes the Nigerian Nightmare!"

A nickname was born and a Kansas City sports legend was about to emerge. In his first NFL game he carried the ball 21 times for 105 yards. When Marty Schottenheimer took over the team in 1989, he made Okoye the heart and soul of the Chiefs offense, and the always-smiling gentleman from Nigeria responded.

"I loved to carry the ball for Marty," Okoye said, smiling. "He called it smashmouth football. I liked that."

Okoye was a one-man highlight reel. Who could forget his 143-yard game against Atlanta, a 153-yard *Monday Night Football* effort against Miami, or a sizzling touchdown run against Seattle in which seven Seahawks bounced off his rock-hard body?

Sports Illustrated's Peter King described the play this way: "He shrugged off an arm tackle from linebacker Tony Woods and churned over linebacker David Wyman, who was flat on his back at the 11. Safety Nesby Glasgow and end Jeff Bryant had shots and missed. Cornerback Patrick Hunter and safety Eugene Robinson dived at Okoye's legs at the 5 and he pistoned through them. At the goal line, cornerback Melvin Jenkins made a fruitless grab for him. Seven Seahawks had tried to stop Okoye and seven had failed."

Former teammate Bill Maas wonders what Okoye might have accomplished had he grown up with the game. "If he really knew about the game, had that sixth sense that allows the great backs to find the openings, he might have been the best ever," the former defensive lineman said. "As it was, he survived on brute power. He just ran over people. No one—and I mean no one—wanted to ever get hit by him in practice."

Former center Tim Grunhard echoed that comment.

"If you got hit by Christian from behind, it was like getting hit by a battering ram," Grunhard said. "He'd hit you harder than the opposing defensive linemen. But the man was a player. He was so much fun to block for because you knew if he got any type of opening, he would do the rest."

Unfortunately for Okoye, injuries began taking their toll on his 6'3", 260-pound frame and he underwent surgery before the start of the 1993 season.

"In 1993 the Chiefs signed Joe [Montana] and Marcus [Allen] and I wanted so badly to play with them," Okoye said. "But I had the surgery and was placed on injured reserve and that was it."

He retired at age 32, and felt some bitterness toward the Chiefs for the way they handled his final injury. But that bitterness is now gone; he is a frequent visitor to Kansas City and always attends the annual Chiefs Reunion Game.

"The Chiefs gave me the opportunity to prove I could play professional football and I feel blessed because of that," he said. "I love Kansas City very much."

The first player in the history of the Kansas City Chiefs to lead the NFL in rushing (1,480 yards in 1989) capped his short but brilliant career by earning a spot in the Chiefs Ring of Honor.

THE "WILL" TO SUCCEED

Numbers have always played an important role in professional sports. Hallowed numbers like 56 (Joe DiMaggio's record hitting streak) and 511 (Cy Young's career wins) are significant in baseball; 100; (Wilt Chamberlain's single-game record) represents greatness in the NBA; and 49 (Peyton Manning's single-season touchdown mark) is the number all quarterbacks chase in the NFL.

Numbers tell a part of Will Shields's story as well. There is the number 223—the number of consecutive starts for the 12-time Pro Bowl performer. There is the number 2003—the year he was named the NFL's Man of the Year. There is also the number 2005—the year he and his wife, Senia, were named Philanthropists of the Year by the Kansas City Council.

But think about this number for a moment: 100,000. That is the number of individuals who have been helped by Shields's Will to Succeed Foundation, which benefits centers for abused and neglected women and children.

When asked what number was special to him, Shields smiled and said, "One. When I came to Kansas City back in 1993, my goal was to help one person. If I could have achieved that goal, I would have been very happy." Now, he can magnify that happiness by 100,000.

"I have had the distinct pleasure of witnessing first hand the involvement Will and Senia have had in the community," said team president and CEO Carl Peterson, who encourages every player to get involved in a community project. "Simply put, they have done everything the right way. Of all the players we have had here in my 15 years, I don't know of any individual and his wife who have contributed so much and in so many ways."

Trent Green looks downfield for a receiver as teammate Will Shields (left) blocks Tampa Bay's Anthony McFarland in a November 2004 game.

While the Will to Succeed Foundation is one of the most respected charitable organizations in the state, Shields also served on the board of directors of the Marillac Center and was the Chiefs' United Way spokesperson in 2003.

"When I came here, 17 guys on the team had a foundation. I wanted to do something to help, and I wanted to get totally involved. I didn't just want to lend my name or my face."

Now his foundation has almost overshadowed his accomplishments on the playing field. So, Will, how do you have time to play football? Again, he grins. It's the type of smile that can warm a room and make any visitor feel comfortable.

"I enjoy the game. I enjoy getting prepared for the game. I enjoy practices. I enjoy everything about it," Shields said after a recent practice session. "And I know that because I am an NFL player, in a community that loves and supports its team, I can have a voice and people will listen."

Shields is considered to be the best right guard and the finest all-around lineman in the league. But when his teammates talk about him, they rarely mention his prowess on the football field. When asked about Shields, fellow Pro Bowl performer Tony Richardson said, "How much time do you have? I can fill that notebook talking about Will. He is amazing, one of the most amazing men I have ever met. He is an amazing athlete—the way he has played 12 years and never missed a game, or even a practice, is remarkable. But as good as he is on the field, he's an even better person."

"I don't know of many people who have done more for their community than Will and Senia. I mean it when I say this, it is an honor to have him as a teammate and a friend." Quarterback Trent Green adds, "Will Shields is pure class, on and off the playing field."

And former coach Dick Vermeil raves about the veteran lineman. "He's just so smart, and you know he's going to be out there every Sunday. He's a rock."

Shields's consecutive start streak almost ended in 2000 when he had a bad hamstring and an ankle sprain. "I didn't know if I could go in the pregame," Shields said. "I was warming up, but I didn't feel too good. But Grunny [former center Tim Grunhard] was hobbling around and it didn't look like he was going to play, so I went out there. I played. That's just part of the game. You're always sore and hurting—some days are just worse than other days."

There were all sorts of rumors regarding whether or not Shields would return for his 13th season. "My body will tell me when it's time to quit," he said. "Well, my body and my teammates. I got a lot of calls from guys this off-season wanting to know if I was coming back. That made me feel good—to know they still respected me and wanted me to come back. Plus, I'm pretty competitive. I enjoy playing the game. I'm driven by the competition. My wife and I can't really play board games against each other because we're so competitive—neither one of us like to lose."

So how does this mountain of a man, who has been a rock in the Chiefs' offensive line and the Kansas City community, feel about the fact that he has yet to play in a Super Bowl? "I think about that," he said. "I would love to play in a Super Bowl. That is one reason I came back this year. It is my one and only goal every year. But can I walk away from the game and still be fulfilled if we don't reach the Super Bowl this season? The answer to that is yes. And when I walk away, I will walk away because I know the time is right. It's not going to be a woulda, coulda, shoulda thing.

"I love what I do, I love my teammates and this community, but I want to be able to play with my kids and be able to enjoy life after football. I know the time is near. And I am lucky enough to be in a position where I can make that final decision."

DANTE'S INFERNO

Dante Hall glanced skyward. Micah Knorr's punt was sailing toward him. The most electrifying player in the NFL grabbed the ball near the 7-yard line, looked at the wall of Denver special-team players, and began to retreat.

"That was a bobo play," Hall said. "That should have been a fair catch. The coaches tell me to be smart and the first part of that return was not smart. I think I caught it on the 8, went back to the 5, then to the 2, and back even farther. I just kept getting dumber and dumber and dumber. Ohhh, I've got to get out of this jam."

He did. For the fourth week in a row, Hall returned a kick for a touchdown. Traded to the Rams in the off-season, St. Louis fans will now be able to appreciate Hall's electric returns.

"People have heard me say that Dante would return a kick for a touchdown when everything doesn't go perfectly," Coach Vermeil said. "Maybe this was the return."

Hall juked two defenders inside the 5-yard line, darted past three more between the 5- and 15-yard lines, and then had to let Mike Maslowski take care of Knorr to create a wide-open field.

"When it comes down to the punter," Maslowski said, "you can bet Dante's going to score."

Maslowski knocked Knorr halfway to Raytown and the celebration began. The press box even exploded with applause. People were cheering and high-fiving each other.

ESPN analyst and former Chiefs quarterback Ron Jaworski said, "That's the greatest return I've ever seen in my life. It's the play of the year in the NFL. It's amazing!"

And this guy watches more film than Ebert and Roeper combined.

As Hall left a postgame press conference, a group of visitors broke into applause.

"I was beside myself, so excited for him," Vermeil said. "I was just hoping they didn't call some kind of penalty on us for being too excited or showing too much enthusiasm for what he just did. He's playing with a lot of confidence and toughness."

And he's putting Chiefs special-teams players on the NFL map.

"I don't know how guys tackle him," special-teams member Monty Beisel said. "We're blocking for him and we know what way he's supposed to go."

Maslowski agreed. "I look up and there are five or six guys ready to tackle him," Maslowski said, "and then you see him take off and he's going for another touchdown. I don't know how he does it."

Hall had some extra motivation during the game. Former Texas A&M teammate Chris Cole said in a Denver newspaper that the Broncos would shut down Hall.

"Now that the game is over, I'm going to blow his phone up every day," Hall said, grinning.

Hall poked a little fun at his teammates, too.

"There were a lot of guys in the locker room claiming a great block," Hall said, laughing. "I can't wait to see the return [on film] and see who was actually telling the truth."

What he'll see is the most exciting one-man show in the NFL.

JUST CALL THESE UNLIKELY FRIENDS THE CHIEFS' "ODD COUPLE"

Kansas City Chiefs owner Lamar Hunt calls him "a member of our family." Kansas City Mayor Kay Barnes calls him "a real treasure."

Baseball Hall of Famer George Brett calls him "the one guy you need to call if you're having a charity function in Kansas City."

All-Pro return man Dante Hall said, "He's more than a friend, more like a second father."

Who are these Kansas City luminaries talking about?

Kansas City's Mr. Music, Tony DiPardo.

Since 1963 DiPardo has been the bandleader for the Kansas City Chiefs. Late coach Hank Stram thought enough of DiPardo to honor him with a Super Bowl ring. At the tender age of 92 DiPardo opened the 2004 Indy Racing League race at the Kansas Speedway by playing the national anthem before a televised audience of more than 4 million and a sold-out crowd of 80,000.

"Can you imagine?" DiPardo asked. "A poor little Italian kid from St. Louis has all these good things happen to him? I pinch myself and I still feel like I am dreaming."

"I've played with greats like Sammy Davis Jr., Andy Williams, and Sonny and Cher," DiPardo said, "but I can't think of anything I've enjoyed more over the years than playing for 80,000 fans every Sunday at Arrowhead Stadium." It wasn't always like that, as the Chiefs once played to a mere handful of fans at old Municipal Stadium at 22nd and Brooklyn in downtown Kansas City.

"We needed someone the fans knew, someone they were familiar with, so we hired Mr. Music to be our music director," the late Hunt said. "We sealed the deal with a handshake, and have done so every year since. I don't think there's anyone in the history of the league who has worked for one team longer than Tony. He's very special."

He's also a dreamer.

"I dream a lot, and I pray a lot," said the energetic DiPardo, who greets everyone with a warm smile and a good, old-fashioned Italian hug. "It just amazes me that so many of my dreams have come true. And all of my prayers have been answered. I have been on this earth for 92 years, and I consider myself the luckiest man alive. I have my beautiful wife and partner of 65 years, Doddie, and our wonderful family. God has blessed me with good health so that I can still take a deep breath and blow a 'CHARGE' on my trumpet and lead the Kansas City Chiefs to another victory. I have been blessed with a lifetime of memories and I want to share them with everyone."

DID YOU KNOW...

The Chiefs played the Buffalo Bills in the first-ever game at Municipal Stadium on August 9, 1963. They won 17–13 before a crowd of 5,721.

Whether he is on the bandstand at Arrowhead Stadium or having dinner at a local restaurant, Chiefs fans keep coming up and asking DiPardo the same question:

"DiPardo, how did you become such good friends with Dante Hall?"

It's a question DiPardo loves to answer.

"I love to answer it almost as much as I love Dante," he said, his eyes dancing. "He is the most special player I've met in the 41 years being associated with the Chiefs. I don't why, or really how, our friendship got started, but it's grown and developed over the past few years to the point that I consider him a member of my family."

On December 8, 2002, the Chiefs were playing St. Louis. It was a big rivalry game and everyone was talking about how the Rams were the best team in the state.

"Well, they weren't the best team in the state on that day," Mr. Music said. "And my good friend Dante Hall played one of the biggest roles in the Chiefs' 49–10 victory. I didn't even know Dante before that game. I'd read about him and watched him play the previous season, but I didn't know him. Anyone who has ever been to a Chiefs game, with little doubt, knows that I get very excited when the Chiefs score a touchdown or make a big play. But on this particular cold December afternoon, the old man got so excited that my toes tingled and the hair stood up on the back of my neck."

Hall returned a kickoff 86 yards for a score. The Chiefs' long-time musical director was sitting in his chair with a Chiefs blanket over his legs, just watching the play, when Hall broke free. DiPardo jumped out of his chair as Hall crossed the end zone and handed him the ball.

"I was so shocked! I couldn't believe it!" he said. "Dante was giving the ball to me! I'd seen players spike the ball, slam it like a basketball over the goal post, toss it to some fans, or hand it to an official, but never had I personally been on the receiving end of getting a football after a touchdown. I didn't know what to say or do. I was speechless.

"I just stood there and looked up in the stands and all the fans were cheering. Of course, they were cheering for Dante. But then they began cheering for the old man, and I just felt so happy and excited. It was a feeling that started in my heart and then went through my body like a rocket. I showed the ball to my daughter, Patti, and we were hugging, and the guys in the band were giving me high fives, and I just couldn't stop thinking about Dante. Why on earth would someone like Dante Hall even think of an old guy like Tony DiPardo?"

The Chiefs' music legend soon found out that the Pro Bowl return man knew more about him than he knew about himself.

"I'm a guy who likes to do his research," Hall said, sporting an easygoing smile. "When I got to Kansas City I wanted to know everything about the community, about the team, about the fans—you name it, I found out about it. While I was doing that research, I kept reading the name Tony DiPardo. I asked people about him and I found out that he was much more than the Chiefs band leader. He'd played with Sammy Davis Jr. and he toured all over the country with his big band back in the heyday of big band music during the '30s and '40s. He was a guy I wanted to meet, to talk with. And I thought to myself, 'If I ever get the chance to meet him, we're going to hang [out] and talk music.'

"When I ran that touchdown back against the Rams, I was heading into the end zone and I saw Tony. He was in front of the bandstand and his arms were up in the air like he was really celebrating, really happy for me," Hall said. "It wasn't planned. I never thought about it once before the game or during the run, but I just ran over and handed him the ball. I could have given it to a fan, or saved it for myself, but I'll never forget the smile on his face when I gave it to him. I think he was about the happiest person I ever saw."

Chiefs Hall of Fame broadcaster Dawson felt much the same way as he called the play from his radio suite in the Arrowhead Stadium press box.

"Now you have to remember that I've known Tony for more than 40 years," Dawson said, "and I could see how thrilled he was from way up in the press box. While I was broadcasting the game, I wondered why Dante would give Tony the ball. Like everyone else in the stadium, I wondered if they were good friends. Talk about an odd couple—a 20-something kid from Texas and a 91-year-old Italian who is a Kansas City icon.

"After the game, I went down on the field to do my report and as I walked in the 50-yard-line tunnel to the field, Tony was walking up from the field, and he was holding that football like it was a newborn baby. I went up to him and said, 'Tony, I just talked to Dante and he wants that football back.' I was just joking—but the look of horror on Tony's face kind of scared me. I thought, 'Oh, my God, I've caused Tony DiPardo to have a heart attack.' I told him I was just kidding, and you could see the relief just wash over his entire body. He smiled and showed me the ball and told me that he was going to ask Dante to autograph it."

After the next home game, DiPardo went up to the locker room and asked one of the guards if he would ask Hall to come out into the waiting area near the stadium elevators. A minute later, the security guard came back and said that Hall was in getting treatment.

"He had been hit really hard that game. So I reluctantly asked the security guard if he would take the ball back in to Dante and ask him to sign it for me," DiPardo said. "A couple of more minutes passed when all of a sudden the locker room door opened, and there was Dante. I was so surprised and delighted. Standing there in nothing more than a towel because he was getting treatment ... he wanted to personally meet me and sign the ball in person. Wow! He invited me into the locker room and he had me sit in his chair. Imagine that, me sitting in his chair in front of his locker. He told me about his love of music and how he appreciated everything I had done in the music business and we just hit it off."

A smile comes to Hall's face when that moment is mentioned.

"I didn't come to Kansas City looking for a 91-year-old friend," Hall said, shaking his head and laughing. "But I have one with Tony. I don't care if he's 91 or 191. He's my friend and he's one of the most special people in my life. When I saw how excited he was after I gave him that ball, I made a vow to myself that every time I scored a touchdown, he was going to get the ball. I told him he was going to have to build a trophy case in his house for all the balls."

And that's exactly what DiPardo has done.

"And I don't just have the balls Dante has given me, I've had them designed with photos of Dante, the score of the game, the date—they're made up just beautiful and then Dante signs them for me. The first thing I do whenever a guest comes over to our house is bring them down to my office and show them all my footballs. I still have to pinch myself to think that a player like Dante Hall—a Pro Bowl player with hundreds of thousands of fans—would think about the old man and give him the touchdown balls.

"It's like I said, I dream a lot. But I could never have dreamed about someone like Dante doing something this special for me. Now, I say a little prayer for Dante—not about him scoring a touchdown—but about him playing strong and avoiding any injuries. I pray for all the special people in my life. I want all of them to be safe and happy and as full of love as I am."

JOHNSON STARS WHEN GIVEN THE OPPORTUNITY

For three seasons Larry Johnson was the Kansas City Chiefs version of an angry young man. He knew he had the skills that were necessary to become a star in the NFL, but he had to sit on the bench and wait for his time to come. He grimaced when he looked at his stats—six games played in 2003 with no starts, three starts and 10 games played in 2004, and then came that magical 2005 campaign in which the young man whose maturity had been challenged by his head coach finally got the opportunity to strut his stuff.

After three years of waiting in the wings, Larry Johnson made the most of his opportunity and is now one of the top three rushers in the game.

The Chiefs made the former 2,000-yard back from Penn State their number one draft pick in 2003 because All-Pro Priest Holmes was coming off a serious hip injury and there was some doubt about his ability to return to action.

Johnson appreciated the fact that he could sit and learn from the best, but when coach Dick Vermeil gave Derrick Blaylock the chance to start when Holmes was on the sideline, Johnson lost his cool.

"I just wanted to play, to get the chance," Johnson said.

That chance came in 2005, when Holmes suffered a serious neck injury and the Chiefs placed the ball in the hands of Johnson, who responded with nine consecutive 100-yard games and earned a spot on the AFC Pro Bowl team.

Johnson told Cris Carter on HBO's *Inside the NFL* that he and Vermeil didn't have a very good relationship. "I wouldn't pay attention. My eyes, I would be up in the sky. You know, I would be sleeping in my locker. I wouldn't carry my playbook because I was just trying to get away from this building, you know, when Dick was here."

He went on to say that his relationship with new head coach Herm Edwards was much better.

"I can relate to Herman. I couldn't do that with the other coaches I had because they had not done it. You know, they haven't put [on] those pads or they haven't been in the situation as a young black athlete and know what we had to go through."

When Edwards replaced Vermeil, the first thing he did was call Johnson into his office, where he told him that he would be the featured back in 2006.

"He kind of looked at me with this 'Are you messin' with me?' look, and I had to assure him that I wasn't messin' with him," said Edwards. "He was going to be my running back. If we needed him to carry the ball 30 times a game, we were going to place it in his hands 30 times."

While Johnson savored the challenge, it was apparent that it might be difficult to follow in the steps of Holmes, who had set the single-season touchdown record and broken nearly every Chiefs rushing record in a six-year span. Then left tackle Willie Roaf announced his retirement before the start of the season and quarterback Trent Green went down with a concussion in the first game and would miss eight games. All the offensive focus shifted to Johnson.

"I like a challenge, and I always said I just wanted the chance to prove what I can do," Johnson said, "and Herman gave me that chance."

Johnson followed up a 1,750-yard 2005 campaign with 1,789 yards, 17 touchdowns, and a trip to the playoffs. He was named a member of the AFC Pro Bowl for the second year in a row and seems like a man content with his place on the Chiefs.

"He's matured," Edwards said. "He was always a great kid. We just needed to bring him along and give him the chance to prove what he can do. That's all he ever wanted."

JOHNSON NEEDS NO MOTIVATION

Memo to the Kansas City Chiefs from running back Larry Johnson: "I don't need no motivation. If I need motivation, I'll talk to my father. I don't need another grown man telling me I need to take the diapers off."

That remark came from the former Kansas City Chiefs number one draft pick, who was steamed when then-coach Vermeil said that Johnson—needed to "take the diapers off" and prepare for a possible start if the injured Priest Holmes could not answer the call.

"That's not how I've been raised, and I don't need no motivation from anybody. I'm self-motivated because my father taught me to be that way," Johnson fumed.

Johnson's father is Larry Johnson Sr., the defensive line coach at Penn State University, where his son became just the second back in the history of the Big 10 to rush for more than 2,000 yards his senior season.

At the time, Vermeil was not a big fan of Johnson. But he did backtrack a bit when asked about the comment, telling the Associated Press, "It just popped into my scrambled head.

"He's got some pressure on him now because if Priest doesn't play, he's going to be carrying a load, and it's a lot of responsibility that so far he has a way to go to prove he can handle it. And I'm looking forward to giving him the opportunity if Priest can't play."

Vermeil added that the comment was made in jest, but "in a way, there's a little truth to it."

"I like Larry and I see his talent. And I've spent more time with Larry Johnson than all my roster combined in the last two years, and so has everybody else in this building. And sooner or later, he's going to recognize that."

Sooner or later, maybe, but not in 2004.

"Yes, it's a little frustrating when they bring you here and they can't tell you whether you're going to play or you're not going to play," said Johnson, who had to wait three years to start at Penn State.

"That's just how I feel. By no means I'm going to stop going hard here and going hard every day in practice. It's just something that's frustrating right now and would be to anybody who's in my position."

That's a part of Johnson's frustration that his coach understands and appreciates.

"The kid wants to play football. He loves to play," Vermeil said. "But in this league, they just don't automatically retire Priest Holmes."

"He has all the talent in the world," Vermeil said of Johnson, "and sooner or later, he'll have his opportunity to take advantage of it."

Truer words were never spoken.

GREEN BECOMES QUIET TEAM LEADER

Okay, NFL trivia experts: between 2001 and 2004, what NFL quarterback threw for the most yards? If you said Peyton Manning, light up a cigar and pat yourself on the back. The man who led the Indianapolis Colts to a victory in Super Bowl XLI threw for 17,155 yards.

If you know who the number two passer was during that same period, then you really are a fan.

Tom Brady?

Nope.

How about Brett Favre?

Sorry.

Try Trent Green, the Kansas City Chiefs starting quarterback who saw a dream season in St. Louis come to an end on a wicked tackle by San Diego's Rodney Harrison. That injury kept him on the sideline while an unknown former Arena League quarterback named Kurt Warner led the Rams to a Super Bowl title.

Between 2001 and 2004 Green threw for 16,103 yards.

"I don't look at the yards or the touchdowns or anything like that," said Green, who has become the rock-solid leader of the Kansas City Chiefs offense. "I look at consistency. That's what is important to me because that's what produces victories."

Green dropped down to fourth (following Manning, Favre, and Brady) in passing yards between 2001 and 2006 because he was knocked unconscious by Cincinnati's Robert Geathers in the first game of the 2006 season and missed eight games.

Green was running for a first down when Geathers drilled him as he began his slide. Geathers's shoulder pads hit Green up high and he violently crashed into the Arrowhead Stadium turf. Green was unconscious for several minutes, waking up just before the ambulance arrived at a Kansas City hospital.

"When I came back, I didn't play with any fear," Green said, "just because of some of the things I've been through early in my career. No, you can't play the position with fear, and I don't anticipate doing that."

However, after losing his job to Warner in St. Louis, Green said there was some concern about regaining his starting job.

"There's always concern, especially since it's happened to me before," he said. "So there's always concern, but I have confidence in what I do. I had confidence in myself in '99 that when I came back and had an opportunity to play, that I'd play well. It was nothing against Kurt. He played great, and obviously was the league MVP. But it didn't make me think any less of myself and I think that's something you have to have."

"Trent came back, got popped, and it's like, 'I'm glad it's over,'" Coach Edwards said. "He's a pro's pro, a man. Sure, it's going to be in the back of his mind, but it's not going to affect him."

Green had to deal with something much more serious in 2005 when his father Jim passed away on October 27.

"I'd never played a game at Arrowhead without my dad there," Green said. "That was very difficult."

Long before any of the fans had arrived, Green walked up to his father's seat and videotaped a tribute to his father and number one fan. Some Arrowhead security guards watched Green and then assured the grieving quarterback that no one would sit in his father's seat.

Green then went into the locker room and prepared mentally to face the Oakland Raiders, knowing that left tackle Roaf, Pro Bowl running back Holmes, cornerback Patrick Surtain, and reserve defensive backs Jerome Woods and Dexter McCleon would all miss the game with injuries.

"We knew we had our leader, Trent Green," defensive back Greg Wesley said, "and we'd follow him anywhere. The guy just lost his father and comes into the game and leads us to the winning touchdown as time expires. Now, that's a leader."

Despite having that galaxy of stars watching from the sideline, the Chiefs somehow managed to pull out a thrilling 27–23 win when Larry Johnson, starting in place of Holmes, scored the winning touchdown from one yard out as time expired.

"I loved the call," Chiefs defensive end Jared Allen said when asked about coach Dick Vermeil's decision to go for the winning touchdown, rather than the chip-shot field goal. "I'm on the sideline like, 'Yeah! Go for it!' And when we did, I got pretty excited."

So did left guard Brian Waters, who was blocking on the game-winning run.

"We needed to win this game," Waters said. "I was just so proud of every member of this team. The secondary was all beat up and look what they did and we came through with three late scores and get a big win. This is huge."

That's what Trent Green means to the Kansas City Chiefs.

After Johnson scored the game-winning touchdown, Green knelt on the Arrowhead turf and pointed to the heavens. Tears ran down his face as he embraced coach Dick Vermeil on the sideline.

"You want to know what leadership is?" asked Vermeil after the game. "What Trent Green did today, that's leadership."

NUMBERS DON'T LIE

MARTY AND CARL

Lamar Hunt is a smart man. As he gazed out of his suite at Arrowhead Stadium he realized two things: first, numbers don't lie. Second, neither did the countless number of empty seats at Arrowhead Stadium.

After a thrilling roller-coaster ride of success with the Dallas Texans and Kansas City Chiefs, Hunt's team had become the laughing stock of the league. The period from 1975 to 1988 was simply known as "the Dark Ages."

A running joke in Kansas City went something like this: a man left two Chiefs tickets on the dashboard of his car and went into a convenience store to pick up some milk and a loaf of bread. He'd left his window down and thought to himself, "I hope those tickets are still there when I get back to my car." When he paid for the items, he returned, and there, sitting on his dash, was another pair of tickets.

The man who told that joke was Kansas City Chiefs nose tackle Bill Maas, who later said, "You couldn't give a Chiefs ticket away. If you asked someone if they wanted a ticket, they looked at you like you were crazy."

Want to talk about numbers? In his 14 years with the Chiefs, Hank Stram was 124–76–10. After he was fired following a 5–9 record in 1974, the next five Chiefs coaches were a combined 81–128–1.

Hunt shouldered the blame for the demise of the Chiefs, saying, "I gave Hank too much responsibility when I made him general manager and director of scouting after we won the Super Bowl. There was a period when we didn't do a good enough job of scouting and bringing in new players. I blame myself for letting that happen."

During Frank Gansz's final, disastrous season as the Chiefs head coach, when they limped home with four victories, Carl Peterson—the player personnel director of the Philadelphia Eagles—sat in the stands at Arrowhead Stadium and gazed at the more than 40,000 empty seats; the Chiefs were off to a 1–8–1 start. Peterson had been asked to attend a Chiefs game during the 1988 season to give owner Hunt his honest opinion on the state of his team. Arrowhead was a state-of-the-art facility that was basically empty on most Sunday afternoons from October through November.

The Chiefs had employed three coaches during the 1980s and none of them could find the key to success. A player strike led to the firing of Marv Levy (who went on to take the Buffalo Bills to four Super Bowls), John Mackovic's arrogance did him in, and the energetic Gansz found that although he was a special, special teams coach, that didn't translate to getting the job done as the head man.

One day after the 1988 season came to an end, Hunt hired Peterson to be the Chiefs general manager, president, and CEO. It was a daunting task and Peterson knew he had to find the right coach if he ever wanted to lead the Chiefs out of the wilderness and into the bright sun that always seemed to shine over winning programs.

Marty Schottenheimer, who had come so close to leading the Cleveland Browns to two Super Bowl appearances only to see those dreams crushed by John Elway and the Denver Broncos, had had a falling out with Browns owner Art Modell and was looking for a change in scenery.

Peterson, who had been an assistant coach before taking a front-office job with the Philadelphia Eagles, was a longtime fan of Schottenheimer's and hired him to be the architect of a new

Coach Marty Schottenheimer (right) shares a laugh with team president Carl Peterson before a January 1998 game.

plan in Kansas City. Peterson made changes on the field, on the sideline, and in the front office. He wanted to make a game at Arrowhead Stadium an event, but he also knew that the product on the field would play the most important role in the resurrection of a once-proud franchise.

"This team has an excellent tradition of winning," Schotteneheimer said, "and I don't see why we can't rekindle it."

Added Peterson, "They wanted to sign me to a five-year deal, but I said no. If we can't create a winner here in four years, it's time for someone else to have a shot."

In their first season together, the Chiefs finished with an 8–7–1 record—that's four wins more than the previous year. They made linebacker Derrick Thomas their first pick and he proved to be the most exciting linebacker to wear the crimson and gold since a guy named Willie Lanier.

Peterson brought in veteran players like center Mike Webster, who tutored a kid from Notre Dame named Tim Grunhard, and quarterbacks Ron Jaworski and Steve DeBerg. They gave the team leadership and instant creditability.

New vice president of administration Tim Connolly sent out a flyer to fans and asked what they missed or what they wanted at the stadium; the overwhelming reply was the return of former bandleader and Kansas City icon Tony DiPardo. The Chiefs brought back their legendary bandleader, who had stepped away because of illness. He had been with the team since it arrived in Kansas City, and the fans welcomed him back with open arms.

The Chiefs cracked down on fan rowdiness, promised a more wholesome and cleaner atmosphere, and the end result was a 23 percent boost in season ticket sales.

Peterson was the ying to Schottenheimer's yang. Over a 10-year stretch, they were not only the most successful GM and coach pair in the league, they were the longest-lasting duo in a league that casts aside coaches and front-office personnel like yesterday's trash.

While the Marty and Carl Show never achieved the ultimate goal of reaching a Super Bowl, they brought respectability back to One Arrowhead Drive and made it the place to be.

"More than anything else," Peterson said, when asked about the Arrowhead experience, "I love the atmosphere. People plan their tailgating parties weeks in advance and they make a day out of it. Our fans are a big reason for our success and I always want them to be aware of that. I think the best thing you can say about Arrowhead Stadium is that opposing teams hate to play here. You can't get a better compliment than that."

By the way, if you want to crunch some more numbers, no team in the AFC had more fans attend their home games than the Kansas City Chiefs during the 1990s. The Dark Ages were over. And, so too, was the Marty Schottenheimer/Carl Peterson era. It came to an end January 11, 1999. Schottenheimer, who posted a 101–58–1 record in his 10 years with the Chiefs, knew it was time to move on and left with the class and dignity he had displayed as coach for the past decade.

THOMAS PAVED THE WAY TO CHIEFS' RETURN TO GLORY

It's not coincidental that general manager Carl Peterson, coach Marty Schottenheimer and their first-ever number one draft pick,

Alabama linebacker Derrick Thomas, all arrived at the same time as the team's fortunes began to spiral upward.

Following a disastrous stretch during the mid 1970s through the entire decade of the 1980s, the Chiefs were the doormat of professional football. A coaching merry-go-round that included Marv Levy, John Mackovic, and Frank Gansz provided fans with nothing but futility and made the Chiefs the focal point of late-night comedians.

But all that changed when owner Lamar Hunt cleaned house, bringing aboard Schotteneheimer, Peterson, and the Alabama All-American.

Derrick Thomas was the 1988 Butkus Award winner, named the best linebacker in the college ranks. And he was the one player both Schottenheimer and Peterson coveted. With the fourth pick in the 1989 draft the Chiefs selected the man who would rewrite the team—and NFL—record books. He came to Kansas City with an easy smile, a passion for football, and the will to turn a coma-tose franchise into one of the most successful squads of the 1990s.

"This is a beginning for Marty, me, and the Chiefs," Peterson said upon selecting Thomas in 1989. The team had made just one playoff appearance since 1971, but all that was about to change. Thomas was named the NFL Defensive Rookie of the Year and his teammates named him the winner of the Chiefs' Mack Lee Hill Award as he finished his rookie season with 10 sacks. He also merited the first of nine consecutive Pro Bowl berths, becoming the first Kansas City rookie to make the Pro Bowl since running back Joe Delaney in 1981. He was the first Chiefs outside line-backer to earn a spot in that game since Pro Football Hall of Famer Bobby Bell in 1973.

When he arrived at the Pro Bowl, he found that he had been issued jersey No. 59 instead of his familiar No. 58. The numbered jerseys are handed out through seniority. In true Thomas fashion, he gave his first Pro Bowl jersey to a neighbor back in Independence, Missouri, and said, "You keep this one. I'll keep all the ones with No. 58 on them."

It took the Chiefs only two seasons before they made the play-offs. In just his second season, Thomas set the NFL afire and

Derrick Thomas sacks Denver Broncos quarterback John Elway during a 1989 game. The drafting of Thomas marked the turning of the Chiefs' fortunes.

created fear among opposing quarterbacks as he recorded 20 sacks, the fifth-highest total in NFL history.

Perhaps his finest individual performance came that Veteran's Day, November 11, 2000, when he set an NFL single-game mark of seven sacks in a 17–16 home loss to Seattle. On the final play of the game, Seahawks quarterback Dave Krieg, who would later become a Chiefs teammate, eluded Thomas's grasp and found Paul Skansi alone in the end zone for a game-winning 25-yard score. Thomas had dedicated the game to his father, Robert, an Air Force pilot who lost his life during a mission called Operation Linebacker II in Vietnam.

When presented with the seventh-sack football, Thomas called a friend in the locker room over to his stall and tossed him the football.

"I don't keep anything from a loss," said Thomas, who later added, "I was on a mission today. I read in the paper that Derrick Thomas was in a sack slump."

Thomas rarely dealt with a slump of any kind, as he led the Chiefs in sacks the first four seasons he played with them. In 1991, he became the first linebacker to win the team's MVP Award.

That same year he started the Third and Long Foundation, a nationally renowned reading program for inner-city youths in Kansas City. He spent Saturday afternoons during the regular season reading with youngsters at libraries across the metro area. His enthusiasm sparked the reading habits of countless young students throughout the Midwest.

"As good a player as Derrick was," said his best friend and teammate Neil Smith, "he was an even better person. A lot of guys start programs and the like, and they just lend their name to them. Derrick didn't do that. He went out and read with the kids and showed them how important it was to study and work hard in school. And when Derrick Thomas is telling a kid that, they listen."

Thomas was making a name for himself in the NFL and in his community. He and Smith became one of the most feared pass-rushing tandems in the NFL, paving the way to an AFC West division title in 1993.

The Chiefs made a thrilling run through the playoffs. They upset the red-hot Houston Oilers, who had won 11 straight games, to advance to the first AFC Championship Game in franchise history.

"That was a special season for a lot of reasons," Thomas said. "Joe [Montana] came over to play quarterback, and we had an offense and a defense that really complemented each other. It was a lot of fun. There was no place I'd rather be than Arrowhead Stadium on a Sunday afternoon with the stands full and the fans chanting and doing the Arrowhead chop."

Thomas earned the NFL's Man of the Year Award that season, and the following season his teammates again named him the team MVP.

"For me, my goals are a lot higher than just being a successful linebacker or being All-Pro," Thomas said. "When my career is over, I want people to look back and view me as the best, or one of the two best, to ever play the position."

Thomas's linebacking hero was former New York Giants Hall of Famer Lawrence Taylor. The two became good friends and Thomas commissioned a huge painting for his home featuring him alongside Taylor. Many times, following a practice session or home game, Thomas would visit with buddies who gathered around his locker, comparing his exploits to those of Taylor.

"Well, I don't know if you can really categorize L.T. as a true linebacker because L.T. never dropped in coverage," Thomas chuckled during one such conversation. "L.T. never covered anybody, but that wasn't his thing. His job was to blitz and to create havoc. L.T. went about things in his own way and he was very successful at it."

Their admiration was mutual. Following a rare Giants road game at Arrowhead, the man Thomas referred to as L.T. said, "Derrick is a great linebacker. He is a game breaker, the guy an opposing quarterback always has to be aware of. He's going to be considered one of the best when his playing days are over." Thomas's numbers compare quite favorably to Taylor's. In 13 seasons with the Giants from 1981 to 1993, Taylor played in 184 games, producing 132.5 sacks and 10 Pro Bowl berths. In 11 seasons with the Chiefs, Thomas recorded 126.5 sacks and earned nine Pro Bowl appearances.

There is one category in which the Chiefs did some research to show that D.T. overshadowed the illustrious L.T. It is in the turnover department, where Thomas established Chiefs records with 45 forced fumbles, 19 fumble recoveries, four touchdowns, and three safeties during his career, compared to 33 forced fumbles, 12 fumble recoveries, two touchdowns, and no safeties for Taylor.

"I have not witnessed a more dominating defensive performer than Derrick Thomas," said his former coach, Schottenheimer. "On rare occasions, the performance of a defensive player dictates that an opponent know where he is aligned every snap of the game. They must design their attack accounting for his presence on each play. Failing to account for this player can result in a loss for your team. Derrick was such a player."

Although he produced just 8 sacks in 1995, he was part of the greatest defensive unit in the game. Under the direction of new defensive coordinator Gunther Cunningham, the Chiefs defense led the NFL in scoring defense (15.1 points per game), touchdowns allowed (23), and yards per play (4.3), while ranking second in total defense, permitting only 284.3 yards per game.

The Chiefs finished the year with a franchise-best 13–3 regular-season record, capping that performance with a 26–3 rout of Seattle. The Chiefs allowed Seattle to gain just 89 yards of total offense, the lowest tally in franchise history. Following the game, Thomas and teammate Smith emerged from the locker room for a celebration lap around the stadium to share another AFC West title with their fans. Carrying a Chiefs flag along the way, it was yet another fitting salute from Thomas to those fans who meant so much to him.

Thomas and the Chiefs were back to their dominating ways once again in 1997 as Kansas City captured the AFC West crown with another 13–3 regular-season record. In a thrilling 24–22 home win over the Denver Broncos on November 16, Thomas reached another milestone, getting career sack number 100. That sack came against John Elway, the adversary Thomas had sacked more times than any other quarterback in team history.

"To document it in the record books, that the 100th [sack] came on Elway, makes it more special, because John is one of the best to ever play the game," Thomas said. "We've had some great battles. He's won some and I've won some and I've enjoyed every one of them."

"Derrick was such an impact player, you always had to know where he was on the field," Elway said. "Derrick the football player was a powerful competitor with remarkable talent and aptitude. He epitomized the heart, courage, and spirit it takes to be an outstanding player. More importantly, Derrick Thomas the man was a philanthropist who gave so much to his family and his community."

While the team didn't reach the playoffs in 1998, Thomas started the season with a bang. In the season opener at Arrowhead, he threatened to break his own NFL record by sacking Oakland's Jeff George six times as the Chiefs stopped their archrivals 28–8. Although there would be few highlights during a 7–9 season, Thomas enjoyed a memorable finale when he scored a 44-yard touchdown on a fumble recovery in the 31–24 victory for the Chiefs. That game would be Schottenheimer's final win as a Chiefs coach.

"Derrick spent his entire professional career in Kansas City and it was my good fortune to coach him all but one year," Schottenheimer said. "Arriving in Kansas City as a young man of 22, he distinguished himself not only athletically, but also as a caring and giving person."

In his final season with the Chiefs, Thomas continued to thrive both on the field and in the community. He held the club record in sacks for a seventh time with seven, finishing his career with 126.5 sacks, the ninth-highest total in league history and a Chiefs all-time record. He also concluded his career owning franchise records for career safeties (three), forced fumbles (six), and fumble recoveries (19), while ranking fifth on the club's all-time tackle chart (728).

But the one statistic that had always eluded Thomas finally came to pass in 1999, when he intercepted his first pass during a 34–0 shutout of the Chargers on October 31.

"I finally got one," he said, grinning from ear to ear. "Nobody's getting this ball. This one's mine to keep. It's going home with poppa."

"IT'S TIME TO STEP DOWN"

The Marty Schottenheimer era came to an end January 11, 1999. The veteran Kansas City Chiefs coach announced his resignation in a surprise announcement at Arrowhead Stadium's Arrowhead Club.

"I'm shocked," Chiefs fullback Tony Richardson said. "I'm in a total state of shock. I feel like we've lost the captain of our ship."

Although Schottenheimer, who posted a 101–58–1 record in his 10 years in Kansas City, said at the end of the 1998 season that he "expected to be back next season," he said a conversation he had with his wife, Pat, changed his mind.

"We took some time to evaluate my role in coaching," Schottenheimer said, speaking from a prepared statement, his voice cracking with emotion. "We decided it's time to step down. I came here with a five-year plan, and it became a 10-year plan. It's time to let someone else implement their plan."

Chiefs owner Lamar Hunt lavished praise on his coach, saying, "The past 10 years represent a golden era of Kansas City Chiefs football. While Marty was here we had the second-best record in the NFL [trailing only the 123–37–0 San Francisco 49ers] and the best record in the AFC. We had the third-best home record [62–18] and the fifth-best road record [39–40–1] and we led the league in attendance for the fifth straight year."

Hunt said he asked Schottenheimer to reconsider when he first learned of the coach's intentions.

"I asked him to sleep on it at least twice before he made his final decision," the Chiefs owner said. "And he reiterated to me this morning of his intentions. I think Marty's records will stand the test of time."

Schottenheimer's teams qualified for the playoffs seven times, won three AFC Western Division titles, and appeared in one AFC Championship Game in 1993, with Joe Montana at quarterback.

> ## DID YOU KNOW...
>
> The first football game former All-Pro running back and native of Enugu, Africa, Christian Okoye saw was one he played in at Azusa Pacific College. He attended the California school on a track scholarship.

But his final team finished with a disappointing 7–9 record after going into the regular season with high expectations. There had been much talk of going undefeated in the preseason, but the Chiefs finished by failing to make the playoffs for the second time in three years.

The Chiefs were unable to reach the ultimate goal, playing in the Super Bowl. And that is the former coach's one regret.

"My time here was very enjoyable and very successful," Schottenheimer said. "We had 10 years to try and get it done, and

Marty Schottenheimer reflects as he answers a question during a news conference announcing his resignation as coach of the Chiefs.

we didn't get it done. Now, it's time for someone else to step in and take over."

Chiefs president and general manager Carl Peterson didn't say who the Chiefs had in mind, but said, "The process will begin immediately."

"We are saddened, but so grateful for the past 10 years," said Peterson, who, along with Schottenheimer, formed the longest-running coach and general manger duo of any team in professional sports. "All of you who doubted that we could stay together for that period of time never understood what Marty and I knew all those years—we had a mutual respect for each other and a common goal."

During the difficult 1998 season, rumors had circulated throughout Kansas City about Schottenheimer's personal life. He emphatically denied them, saying, "There have been rumors about my marriage and my personal life. They are absolutely false and untrue."

He glanced at his wife, Pat, who was sitting in the front row of the Arrowhead Club, when he made the statement. Schottenheimer's son, Brian, an assistant coach on his father's staff, added, "He never brings that kind of stuff home with him. [The rumors] are something we never talked about."

When asked about his father's resignation, he said, "I found out about it last night. I was surprised."

So were the other members of the coaching staff.

Jim Erkenbeck, tight ends coach, said he was made aware of the situation Sunday as he watched football on television.

"I heard about it on ESPN," Erkenbeck said with a grin, "and boy, did the phone lines begin to light up. I bet every coach on the staff was on the phone in 15 seconds. We didn't know for sure it was going to happen until Marty told us this morning."

Peterson said the reason he and members of the Chiefs staff chose not to return phone calls over the weekend was because the coach wanted to tell his staff face-to-face of his decision.

Schottenheimer was 8–7–1 in his first year in Kansas City (1989) and experienced just one losing season, the 7–9 mark in 1998. Schottenheimer said leaving after his first losing season was the toughest thing about his decision.

"The most difficult part was that I was leaving on a losing note," he said. "That was the most difficult obstacle in making my final decision."

He left Kansas City with a career mark of 145–85–1.

"I've been in pro football 32 years—14½ as a head coach," he said. "That's a long, long time. I think it's time to take a break. It's time to relax."

He didn't relax long, as he soon signed with the Washington Redskins, where he never achieved the success he did in Kansas City. After a tumultuous 8–8 season in which he spent more time dealing with owner Daniel Snyder than working with his team, Schottenheimer packed his bags and headed for the West Coast.

He had been the head coach of the San Diego Chargers for the past five years, where he led the Bolts to a 47–33 record. Schottenheimer owns a career mark of 200–126–1 and holds the dubious distinction of being the winningest coach in the history of the NFL who has not taken a team to the Super Bowl.

STILL IN SEARCH OF ELUSIVE GOAL

While the Chiefs didn't reach their ultimate goal of the Super Bowl—the one Peterson talked about in 1989 when he took over the reigns of the struggling team—Kansas City did regroup from a late-season slump to award first-year head coach Herm Edwards with a trip to the playoffs in 2006.

There were enough ups and downs to satisfy an elevator operator as the Chiefs reached the promised land with a 9–7 record despite the loss of quarterback Trent Green for eight games (he suffered a concussion in the first game of the season), the retirement of left tackle Willie Roaf, and the arrival of a new head coach who didn't want to be buddies with any of his players. The man who oversaw everything with an astute eye and often provided a shoulder to lean on was Peterson.

After the retirement of a good friend, Dick Vermeil, from his UCLA days, Peterson began the search for a new head coach. He found the right man for the job in Edwards, a former Chiefs scout and assistant coach who enjoyed success in New York City and survived the life-under-the-microscope approach of the Big Apple's media.

While the 2006 campaign was a success, it was also a year of transition.

"Let me say this: any time you change head coaches, you're in a transition," Peterson said. "You just are. When I hired Marty Schottenheimer, there was a transition and it was an emphasis on the defensive side of the ball. When I hired Gunther, it was the same thing. When I hired Dick, it was a transition to the offensive side.

"I knew what I was getting with Herm. We talked about it before he became head coach. We're in a period of transition. He's had his first year now with this football team and a lot of it he inherited. He knows what he wants to do and he expresses to me and our player personnel people where he wants to go. Now he's had a full year of evaluation of his players and certainly has his thoughts and I want those thoughts because he is the captain of the ship. He has his thoughts on how we beat San Diego and Denver and Oakland."

There has been so much talk about the team's shortcomings, despite a trip to the playoffs that ended with a 23–8 loss at Indianapolis. Did Peterson foresee a total makeover of the team?

"We had a fair amount of new players this year," the CEO and president said, "probably close to a third of the football team. Average-wise, it's been my experience there's usually 15 to 17 players. We actually had more than that last year. These are the questions Herm and I are going through right now. Right now the most important thing is to accurately evaluate where a player is in his career, how he played. Is he ascending, plateauing, or descending, and then, based on that, make good decisions going forward."

The Chiefs were the most explosive offensive team in the NFL under Vermeil's guidance. Green developed into a Pro Bowl quarterback, running back Priest Holmes set an NFL single-season record with 27 touchdowns, and the team's offensive line was second to none.

Green struggled through the 2006 season. The line play was mediocre and Holmes has been replaced by the mercurial Larry Johnson, a former number one draft pick who seemed to always be at odds with Vermeil. Johnson mellowed and flourished under Edwards, but the offense seemed stagnant much of the time and the Chiefs were lacking a wide receiver who could spread the defense. Would it be revamped in 2007?

"Specific to revamping the offense," Peterson said, "that's going to be head coach and [offensive coordinator] Mike Solari's decision. I don't get into that. Regarding player personnel, Herm and I together along with our player personnel people and our coaches are in the process of determining who we would like to come back, who we would let go to free agency to see what the market is, and there are some who might not come back."

Certainly the biggest question concerns the future of 12-time Pro Bowl offensive guard Will Shields. Roaf was reported to have talked Shields out of retirement last season; then the future Hall of Fame tackle walked away from the game. His future is as cloudy as that of the team.

"He's been very consistent the last four or five years with me and now with Herm," Shields said. "He's going to make his own decision and has had a marvelous career of 14 years and 12 Pro Bowls. I know he'll say the same thing as he did when he exited the locker room [following the playoff loss to the Colts]: 'I'm going to see how my back is, my arm is, my knee is, and then I'll make a decision.'"

While Peterson and Edwards must make some difficult personnel decisions, they both know that the team's success must overshadow their personal feelings about an individual player.

"The decisions we make on the player personnel side have to not only be for 2007 but also 2008, '09, and '10," he said. "They have to do with cash and cap planning. Collectively, we're going to make decisions for the future of this franchise.

"You know what San Diego, Denver, and Oakland are doing. Do we know what we face in our division? Yeah, because we know them just like they know us. The draft is where it begins, and every successful team in the National Football League has to put their attention there."

The Chiefs enjoyed a successful draft in 2006 despite the fact that the team raised many eyebrows taking defensive tackle Tamba Hali with their first pick. Because Edwards was a one-time scout for the Chiefs, Peterson believes he will add a tremendous amount of insight to this year's college draft proceedings.

"I had this question asked me many times: is this an easier thing for you because you have a coach who has player personnel experience?" Peterson said. "The simple and honest answer is yes. You certainly hope your first pick is a guy that comes in and contributes right away, and Hali did. Tamba Hali is the guy that we evaluated at Penn State and we need to do it again this year and next."

THE DREAM BACKFIELD

JOE COOL

It all ended far too soon. But for two glorious seasons, Joe Cool brought his own special brand of magic to Arrowhead Stadium. Somehow, someway, Kansas City Chiefs president and general manager Carl Peterson lured Joe Montana away from the San Francisco 49ers—a team he had led to four Super Bowl titles—so he could finish his career in Kansas City.

"It was really a remarkable time in the history of the franchise," Peterson said. "We all knew Joe was past his prime, but once he arrived, he proved he could still play the game."

Montana led the Chiefs to the AFC Championship Game in his first season and provided some memorable moments that come close to rivaling those he had created in San Francisco, where he had been known as the "Comeback Kid." Montana was the architect of 31 comeback wins in San Francisco as well as five in Kansas City. He accounted for a victory at Denver that finally put an end to the Chiefs' Mile High Stadium jinx.

"I'd been doing *Monday Night Football* for 27 years, and one of the greatest games we ever had was on October 17, 1994—Denver and Kansas City," said former *Monday Night Football* analyst and football Hall of Famer Frank Gifford. "Joe was 34 for 54 for 393 yards and three touchdowns. And in the final drive he ate up the clock and, with eight seconds remaining, hit Willie Davis with the winning touchdown pass, which left [Denver quarterback John]

113

Elway with no room to come back. It was a flashback for me because it was clear he was running out of gas, but he had this one more performance for us. I've done well over 400 Monday nights, but only a few stick out and that certainly was one. He was brilliant and it was fun to watch. I've always admired the way he handled his life and himself."

After that game, Davis lavished praise on Montana.

"He was so cool and confident," Davis said. "You just knew with Joe in the huddle, things were going to get done. He was an amazing, amazing quarterback."

Perhaps the most memorable tale of Montana's cool came in the 1989 Super Bowl, where the heavily favored 49ers trailed the Cincinnati Bengals late in the fourth quarter. Down by three points with three minutes and 20 seconds left in the game, Montana stood in the huddle and asked tackle Harris Barton, "Isn't that John Candy in the stands?"

He then led the 49ers 92 yards, throwing for the winning touchdown with 34 seconds left.

"There have been, and will be, much better arms and legs and much better bodies on quarterbacks in the NFL," former 49ers teammate Randy Cross said, "but if you have to win a game or score a touchdown or win a championship, the only guy to get is Joe Montana."

Former Chiefs linebacker Derrick Thomas recalled the first time he saw Montana in the locker room, sans uniform. "He looked like a little old man with all these bruises and scars," Thomas said, grinning. "Then, he'd put on the uniform and become Joe Cool. It was quite a transformation."

It was that type of transformation that helped Montana lead the Chiefs to a 27–24 overtime playoff win over the Pittsburgh Steelers in his first postseason appearance for his new team. The Steelers led 17–7 at the half, but Montana rallied the Chiefs with two fourth-quarter touchdowns to knot the score at 24–24.

Facing a fourth-and-goal from the 7-yard line with one minute and 48 seconds to play, Montana found Tim Barnett in the back of the end zone to send the game into overtime.

Joe Montana drops back to pass against the Seattle Seahawks in a November 1994 game.

"We're in the huddle," said wide receiver J.J. Birden, who caught a touchdown pass in the first half, "and Joe is calling the play. He looks right at me and smiles and says, 'Don't you just live for this?' Tim Barnett was like the third option on that pass play, and Joe made it look so easy—like he was going to throw the pass to him all along."

Montana was at his best in the big games. In four Super Bowls, he put up incredible numbers, completing 83 of 122 passes (68 percent) for 1,142 yards with 11 touchdowns and no interceptions. His quarterback rating was 127.8.

Along with the famous Super Bowl drive against Cincinnati, he threw the pass that resulted in "the Catch" by teammate Dwight Clark. That's when a scrambling Montana lofted the ball into the end zone to Clark. The six-yard touchdown pass, with 51 seconds left, gave the 49ers a 28–27 victory over Dallas for the 1981 NFC Championship.

"At his best, when Joe was in sync, he had an intuitive, instinctive nature rarely equaled by any athlete in any sport," Bill Walsh, his San Francisco coach, told ESPN.com.

Montana came into the NFL with a reputation for dramatic wins. In his last collegiate game, at the 1979 Cotton Bowl, he had to fight off hypothermia to rally the Fighting Irish from a 34–12 deficit to a 35–34 miracle victory. His touchdown pass to Kris Haines as time expired is now part of Notre Dame legend.

Although he spent just two seasons in Kansas City, he will always be remembered for that postseason win over Pittsburgh, the dramatic comeback at Denver, and a 24–17 victory over his former 49ers teammates that was witnessed by 79,907 fans in the stands and more than 400 media personnel in a crowded press box.

"It really wasn't that big of a deal," Montana said, looking back at the game. "It was just the second game [of the 1994 season] and I was playing against some former friends and teammates."

Montana was the only one taking that approach. Chiefs owner Hunt called it "the game of the century" and former 49ers coach George Seifert said, "Obviously this is one of the most publicized games and one that stands out a great deal because of all that Joe has done over the years."

DID YOU KNOW...

Gunther Cunningham was born in Munich, Germany.

While Montana starred on offense, completing 19 of 31 passes for two touchdowns, it was Thomas who stole the show. He sacked Montana's protégé, Steve Young, three times, including once for a safety, and won AFC Defensive Player of the Week honors.

"Young is so mobile," Thomas said, "you had to keep your motor running the entire game. You just had to run, run, run after him. It was a fun afternoon."

Marcus Allen, who came to Kansas City the same year Montana arrived to form a dream Hall of Fame backfield, was pumped up after the game.

"The game was exceptional," said Allen, who carried the ball 20 times for 69 yards and scored on a four-yard run. "There was a lot of buildup about the matchup between Joe and Steve Young and I think the game lived up to all the hype."

Young enjoyed a solid afternoon, completing 24 of 34 passes for 288 yards, but it wasn't enough to topple his former mentor.

"I've learned from the master," Young said, "but we just couldn't get it done today."

On April 18, 1995, in a quiet ceremony inside Arrowhead Stadium, Montana announced his retirement at the age of 38. He wanted to be able to wrestle and play with his kids and he was concerned that one more year of pounding in the NFL would rob him of those opportunities.

When it was announced that he was leaving the game, Montana was lauded by some of the biggest names in the NFL.

"In history, there seem to be great people who come around at a certain time. He was one of those. He came at a time when the game of football was changing. Now they call it the West Coast offense, and he was the perfect man for that kind of offense," former Dallas general manager Tex Schramm said.

"Joe Montana was the greatest quarterback I have ever seen. He did everything that everybody else tried to do and made it look easy. In my 20 years of broadcasting, he was the most dominating player I have ever seen," added Hall of Fame coach and football analyst John Madden.

"I sincerely believe that Joe was the toughest and most talented quarterback who ever played the game. He was also one of the funniest people I've ever been around. Everybody knows about his ability as a player, but it was his sense of humor that made the package complete," said former 49ers teammate Charles Haley.

"The accomplishments of Joe Montana are a great part of NFL history. When people think of Joe Montana, they think of leadership, of fourth-quarter comebacks and Super Bowl victories. He will always represent the excellence of the NFL," former NFL commissioner Paul Tagliabue said.

Montana returned to San Francisco—after all, his heart was still there—and enjoyed a retirement celebration unlike any that city had ever seen.

HE WAS A WORK OF ART

Art Still might be in the Pro Football Hall of Fame had he not toiled for the Kansas City Chiefs during the embarrassing '80s.

"I coached [all-time NFL sack leader] Bruce Smith," said former Kansas City Chiefs linebacker and assistant coach Walt Corey, "and I never coached a better one or played with a better one than Art Still."

Still was one of those players who could inspire, or infuriate a coach. While he got along with the cerebral Marv Levy, he often clashed with the arrogant John Mackovic.

"I had fun," said Still, a free spirit who could sometimes be found riding a member of the grounds crew's tractors around the sports complex. "I worked better with some coaches than others, but I always tried to make the game fun."

When he retired in 1987, Still led the team in career sacks with 73. That total stood until a couple of guys named Derrick Thomas and Neil Smith came along.

"I'll gladly relinquish the sack title to those two guys," said Still, who also averaged 100 tackles a year.

ALLEN LEAVES LASTING LEGACY

Marcus Allen can smile about an incident that happened during the 1983 NFL draft. But it was no laughing matter back when he was coming out of USC. Although he had won the Heisman Trophy, set the NCAA single-season rushing record (2,342 yards), and had the most 200-yard rushing games in history (12), coaches and scouts were questioning his speed, durability, and toughness.

"I didn't understand it then," the Kansas City Chiefs Hall of Fame running back said, "and I still don't understand it."

His coach at USC, John Robinson, did little to quell the criticism when he stated, "I don't see him in the context of a [Walter] Payton or [Earl] Campbell, a dominating player."

When draft day arrived, Allen's worst fears were realized. Darrin Nelson of Stanford and Arizona State's Gerald Riggs were selected in front of Allen, who slipped all the way to the 10th pick, where he was finally tabbed by the Oakland Raiders.

He was furious, but the man who retired with more rushing touchdowns than any other player in the history of the NFL wasn't going to lash out at his critics. He was simply going to prove them wrong.

He earned Rookie of the Year honors in 1982 and went on to claim both NFL and Super Bowl MVP Awards. He once rushed for 100 or more yards in 11 consecutive games, an NFL mark that stood 10 years.

When Allen found himself in Raiders owner Al Davis's doghouse, he began searching for a way out. The man who had dominated his position like few other backs in the league had rushed for 301 and 287 yards during the two seasons before he signed with the Kansas City Chiefs as an unrestricted free agent.

"It was the most humiliating thing I'd ever had to endure," Allen said of his final go-around with the Raiders.

He discovered a new life awaited his arrival in Kansas City. He had always been a favorite of Chiefs coach Marty Schottenheimer, who believed Allen's lack of playing time with the Raiders would prolong his career as a Chief.

"He's easily identified because of his greatness," Schottenheimer said, "his performances in the past. The thing that you have to appreciate about Marcus Allen is that you can place him in the role he has been cast and know there will be no change in the way he works, the way he prepares, the way he is going to set an example for others to follow."

While a member of the Chiefs, Allen became the only man in the history of the NFL to rush for 10,000 yards and catch passes totaling 5,000 yards—no small accomplishment for a player who earned little respect on draft day.

"Achieving that goal was meaningful," Allen said, "because when I first came into the league, there was a string of articles saying I wouldn't be very good, I wouldn't last very long, and would only be an average player."

As the former Houston Oilers coach Bum Phillips said about his prize running back, Earl Campbell, "He may not be in a class by himself, but it don't take long to call roll." The same thing could be said of Allen.

"The value [Allen] brings to this organization cannot equate to dollars," Chiefs president and CEO said of Allen when he signed a contract extension. Allen brought a presence that still lingers in the Chiefs locker room. He brought a style and a class that is missing from today's NFL.

"When Marcus Allen scored a touchdown," fullback Kimble Anders said, "he would hand the ball to the official and trot off the field. He acted like he had been there before."

The antics of some of today's younger players don't sit well with Allen.

"I was pretty quiet when I first came into the league," Allen said. "I knew it was important to keep my mouth shut and prove myself. I thought before I talked. Now I think it is the other way around. It's just a different attitude. You see a different attitude, a changing of the guard."

While he is no fan of showboating or taunting, Allen confesses that he still loves the game.

"The football field is a great place to find out about yourself, to challenge yourself," he said. "There are a tremendous amount of obstacles you must face in your life, and football is the perfect forum for working through them."

ALLEN WALKS AWAY FROM THE GAME HE LOVES

Marcus Allen walked away from the game he had played since he was 10 years old. And that was important to the 38-year-old former Kansas City Chiefs running back. The future Hall of Famer, the man who rushed for more touchdowns than anyone who had ever played the game (at the time of his retirement), was walking—not limping—away from the NFL.

"I clearly thought about that," Allen said during an emotionally charged news conference on April 9, 1998, at Kansas City's Arrowhead Stadium. "One thing I always envisioned was to walk away. It evokes images of Dick Butkus and Joe Namath, who can barely walk. Yes, they're great players. But can they

The classy Marcus Allen looks for daylight as he runs for a 10-yard gain against the San Diego Chargers in a November 1995 game.

really enjoy their lives like they'd like to? That's something I thought about."

Pausing several times to wipe away tears and regain his composure, Allen confirmed reports that he had joined CBS as a football analyst, ending one of the most storied careers in football history.

"I played with love and courage and tenacity. That's all I wanted to do," said Allen, a former league and Super Bowl MVP who appeared in more games (221), rushed for more touchdowns (123), and caught more passes (587) than any other running back in NFL history. His total of 12,243 rushing yards is number ten all time.

"I don't mind crying because I feel I'm happy," he said after Chiefs president Carl Peterson passed him a handkerchief.

Allen, the first running back in NFL history to rush for more than 10,000 yards and catch passes for more than 5,000, had told Chiefs coach Marty Schottenheimer that he would play for another season.

But something happened.

Something that caught Allen off guard.

"The one constant I've had since I came into this league was I could visualize and see plays unfolding, and be a part of that. And frankly, as hard as I tried to create that, the vision wasn't as strong as it needed to be," he said, choking back tears.

He leaves a lasting legacy to both his teammates and opponents.

"He is 'the Man,'" said former Denver safety Dennis Smith. "You can see it in his eyes. He does the intimidating."

Former Oakland Raiders teammate Howie Long said, "I've been around some supposedly tough people and this guy is the real deal. Marcus is the toughest man I've ever been around. You can cut his legs off and he still keeps coming."

Allen was drafted by the Raiders after winning the Heisman Trophy at Southern California in 1981. He was a first-round draft choice and quickly established himself as a superlative runner, blocker, and receiver as well as a powerful locker room presence with uncommon leadership skills. Those qualities weren't lost on Peterson, who signed Allen as an unrestricted free agent in 1993.

"Marcus Allen is the embodiment of the consummate professional football player," Peterson said. "Everything that Marcus did, both on and off the field, was put forth in preparation for giving a winning performance each week."

Allen spent his first 11 years with the Raiders, winning the MVP Award in the 1984 Super Bowl. In 1985, he was the league MVP. But Raiders owner Al Davis forced the team to keep Allen on the bench. Allen even once accused Davis of trying to keep him out of the Hall of Fame. But there was no hint of bitterness as he bid farewell to the game.

"This may seem odd today, but I'd like to thank the Raiders for a wonderful and unique experience ... playing with such great players," he said. "I remember when I was a rookie and Greg Pruitt took me under his wing and told me how to become a great pro."

He had special praise for the Chiefs and Schottenheimer, who signed him at 33 hoping to get at least a couple of playing years.

"Marty, thanks for the opportunity," Allen said, fighting back tears. "To be 33 years old ... to be written off by some, and be given the opportunity just to show what you are and what you do, what I felt like I was born to do, and that was to play football.

"Football has basically been my life. I feel like I'm the luckiest guy alive. You get to live what you want to do. The records, of course, I'm proud of but, my God, it's the people. That's what it's really about."

In closing, he looked at his wife of 10 years, Kathryn, and said, "She has been my teammate, my supporter, and my lover. This is her day."

He then walked away from football, knowing his career was over while realizing he had enough memories to last forever.

DO THE RIGHT THING

GIVING BACK

Malik Jackson sported the wide-eyed look of a youngster who was living a dream. He was shaking hands with Kansas City Chiefs running back Larry Johnson one minute, then stepping to the line and bowling a near strike the next. He was with his two "best friends in the world," Ronnie Sailer and Cardell Miller, and there was enough pizza and soda to fill the Grand Canyon.

The youngsters were having the time of their lives at Lunar Bowl in Blue Springs, Missouri, as Operation Breakthrough thanked its many sponsors by throwing a bowling bash. Operation Breakthrough provides services for the children and families of the inner city, including day care, meals, Children's Mercy Clinic, a dental clinic, speech therapy, play therapy, housing assistance, food and clothing, and social services.

After the event ended, most of those attending went home with their families, but not Malik. The 10-year-old headed back to his homeless shelter. His playmate Ronnie is the adopted son of Sister Berta, the Knute Rockne of Operation Breakthrough.

"Ronnie was adopted when he was an infant," said Sister Berta, who founded Operation Breakthrough 35 years ago. "He was four months old and had already been placed eight times. Eight times. Can you imagine? No child should go through something like that."

She paused amid the merriment and clanking sounds of bowling balls striking pins, "But no child should have to leave an event like this and go to a shelter, either."

No child at the event sported bigger smiles than the three longtime friends who were inseparable throughout the evening.

"I've been with Operation Breakthrough since I was zero," Malik announced, with a touch of pride in his voice.

The comment made Cardell do a double take.

"What I mean is that Cardell has been here since he was one," Malik said. "I was here before I was one, so I say I was here when I was zero."

The youngsters laughed.

"It's a special privilege for me to be with my friends in Operation Breakthrough," Malik said. "I'm never scared when I'm there. Sister Berta makes us all feel special and we get to go to school and learn all kinds of things."

The three youngsters are part of a drum corps that will leave Friday for Anaheim, California, where they will represent Kansas City in its quest to gain All-American City status.

"I didn't even know such a thing existed," Berta said. "We're taking 30 children and we have six chaperones."

A twinkle soon appears in her eyes and she says, "How can you take 30 children to Anaheim and not take them to Disneyland? I made a few phone calls and raised enough money for them to go to Disneyland and have a meal there. And we want each of them to be able to go to the beach and step in the ocean. We want their experience to be special."

DID YOU KNOW...

The Chiefs beat the Bills 22–9 on December 19, 1971, for their last victory at Municipal Stadium. Their famous double-overtime playoff loss to Miami was the last game ever played at the 22nd and Brooklyn site in downtown Kansas City.

TOUCHDOWN NUMBER 100

Marty Schottenheimer had a favorite saying about Hall of Fame running back Marcus Allen.

"Whenever Marcus would score a touchdown," the former Chiefs head coach said, "he would walk over to the official, hand him the ball, and trot back to the sideline. I would tell the young guys on the team, 'That's the way it's supposed to be done. Act like you've been there before.'"

When Allen scored his 100th career touchdown (he retired from the Chiefs as the all-time NFL rushing touchdown leader) in a 24–9 victory the Raiders, he followed a different routine.

"The official came over to get the ball," Allen said, "but I told him I was going to keep that one."

No one could argue with that.

This event was special for everyone, especially Johnson and first-year Chiefs head coach Herm Edwards. When it was announced that Johnson had arrived, Edwards ran up and pleaded, "Mr. Johnson, will you sign my shirt?" The two men laughed and embraced.

Johnson didn't sign that shirt, but he signed everything that was placed in front of him for more than an hour.

"I attended this event last year and I enjoyed it," the soft-spoken Johnson said. "If Coach Edwards is involved in something, I want to be there."

Like Johnson, Edwards posed for several photos and also signed a variety of items. All the while, his wife Lia and 10-month-old daughter Gabrielle mingled with the kids in attendance.

"You know, the young people who attend this event can't afford to see a Chiefs game in person," Edwards said. "But here, they can meet the players, touch them, get to know them. I talk to our players about making a difference in someone's life. And I think they have done that at events like this, and through visiting the kids at Operation Breakthrough."

Moments after bowling a strike, Pro Bowl offensive lineman Brian Waters talked about Operation Breakthrough, which was one of the favorite charities of former Chiefs coach Dick Vermeil and his wife, Carol.

"Something like this gives these kids hope," Waters said as he posed for photos and chatted with sponsors who were bowling on his lane. "There are guys on this team who can't imagine going through what these kids go through every day of their lives. I think we can learn a lot about life through these kids.

"And if we can spend a few hours with them, and give them some hope and help them have a good time, then we will all benefit from it."

David Andre, a board member and committee chairman of the bowling event, said Sister Berta is the backbone of Operation Breakthrough.

"She is an amazing woman," he said. "This began 35 years ago with seven children who needed day care. Today we have 550 kids between the ages of six weeks and 18, and we have a waiting list of more than 800."

Those numbers are overwhelming, but they were of little concern to Malik and Cardell.

"Larry," Cardell asked Larry Johnson, "what car did you drive here tonight?"

Johnson grinned and replied, "The blue one."

The two boys giggled with delight.

As Johnson went back to signing autographs, someone posed a question to Cardell.

Was Johnson his favorite Chiefs player?

"No, Benny Sapp is my favorite," Cardell said. "Larry is just a tad bit behind."

GONZALEZ STARS ON AND OFF THE FIELD

Kansas City Chiefs fans are accustomed to watching Tony Gonzalez on the football field. He is first in Chiefs history with 721 receptions for 8,710 yards and 61 touchdowns and trails Shannon Sharpe (815) for the most receptions in the history of

Tony Gonzalez helps nine-year-old Cardell pick out a radio-controlled car during "Shop with a Jock" in December 2004 in Missouri. The program matches Chiefs players with underprivileged children to buy Christmas gifts.

the league by a tight end. But when fans see Gonzalez sporting a jaunty Santa Claus hat while walking through the aisles of a Wal-Mart store, they are a bit surprised.

They shouldn't be. It was hard to tell who was having more fun—the Chiefs players who were handing out $100 worth of toys to 70 special youngsters or the kids themselves—as Gonzalez hosted his sixth annual Shop with a Jock event in Independence, Missouri.

"I'll tell you who's having more fun," Gonzalez said. "The players. This is an event everyone looks forward to every year."

Gonzalez, who teamed with Wal-Mart to create the event six years ago, said he will never forget one special shopping experience.

"I was out with this little kid and all he wanted was groceries for his family," the perennial Pro Bowl tight end said. "I said, 'Come on, let's get some toys.' And he told me his family needed groceries."

So Gonzalez spent the $100 donation from Wal-Mart on groceries and then dug into his own pocket for a couple of hundred dollars worth of toys for the caring youngster.

"Man, when I was a kid, if someone would have said, 'Here's $100, what do you want?' I'd have bought all sorts of toys. But these kids are pretty special. A lot of them want to get clothes for their moms or brothers or sisters. Those are the kids the guys kind of take care of, if you know what I mean."

Austin, a six-year-old from the Kansas City Chiefs Love Fund, was on a mission.

"Let's go find a Game Boy," he said to monstrous offensive lineman Jordan Black.

Austin's buddy, five-year-old Jaylin, wanted a bicycle.

"Let's check out the bikes first," Black said. "Then we'll go find a Game Boy."

Jaylin tested several bikes before settling on a sporty yellow model with training wheels.

"I better make sure it's all right for you, Jaylin," Black said, grinning.

The 6'5", 310-pound tackle jumped on the bike and rode it down an aisle as Austin and Jaylin laughed in delight.

Several of Gonzalez's teammates joined him on the shopping spree.

"Watching the look on the kids' faces when they find that special toy is better than anything that has ever happened to me on the playing field," said Chiefs fullback Ronnie Cruz, who suffered a broken leg early in the season. "When I broke my leg, I was feeling sorry for myself. Then I see these kids, and watch them get some toys, and it just makes you realize you don't have any troubles at all."

Surprisingly, many of the youngsters didn't know the names of their Chiefs hosts.

"I don't know Tony Gonzalez," eight-year-old Stephen said, "but I do know a guy named Trent Green."

Stephen had a list in hand and needed to find one special gift.

"It's this $50 truck; it's real big," he said, his eyes shining. "It's for my little brother. I don't care what I get as long as I find him that truck."

Have you ever seen a grown man cry? Well, all you had to do was look in the direction of the players, who brushed away

DID YOU KNOW...

Chiefs running back Curtis McClinton scored the first AFL touchdown in Super Bowl history on a seven-yard pass from Len Dawson.

the tears before any of the kids noticed.

Gonzalez is a man who enjoys giving back to the community. He's also a man who will gladly donate an item to the Pro Football Hall of Fame. The jersey he wore January 2, 2005, when he set a single-season record for the most catches by a tight end (102) in a 24–17 loss to the San Diego Chargers, will be waiting for him when he arrives as a member of that elite club.

He also broke the Chiefs mark of 93 receptions that he had set during the 2000 NFL season. His career-high 1,258 yards in 2004 were also the second most receiving yards ever recorded by a tight end in a season. He also joined just four other tight ends in NFL history to register multiple 1,000-yard receiving seasons. The others include Hall of Famers Kellen Winslow and Ozzie Newsome as well as Sharpe and Todd Christensen.

"I'm happy I got the record," Gonzalez said, "but at the same time, it's hard to take satisfaction in getting it in a losing cause. Maybe it's something I'll look back in another week or so and enjoy it then. But right now it's tough to swallow. Maybe some day I can send something to the Hall from a Chiefs victory."

LIVING A DREAM

OUT OF AFRICA

Tamba Hali had a dream. Unlike so many of the other top draft picks who are now playing in the NFL, the Kansas City Chiefs rookie defensive lineman didn't dream of purchasing a home for his mother. He dreamed of purchasing her freedom.

Hali, the Chiefs' number one draft pick in 2006, hadn't seen his mother, Rachel Keita, since he fled war-torn Liberia as a terri-fied 10-year-old. That was 12 years ago. Liberia is still recovering from a 10-year civil war that killed an estimated 300,000 Liberians and displaced another million.

Most of his teenage years were spent trying to keep track of family members, speaking to them occasionally on the phone, trying to keep up with their lives as they survived the warfare and poverty that ripped apart their homeland. All he and his father, Henry Hali, a teacher at Fairleigh-Dickinson University in his family's new home in Teaneck, New Jersey, could think about was finding a way to get Rachel to the United States.

Since their departure from Liberia, Rachel had been wounded by random gunfire and became seriously ill with one of the many diseases that still ravage the area. But Henry had no financial means to get Rachel out.

"I always felt like she was in danger because she was still in a country that's about 80 percent unemployed and is just coming off a war," Tamba said.

The Chiefs' 2006 first-round draft pick, Tamba Hali, meets with reporters following a practice session in May 2006 at the Truman Sports Complex in Kansas City.

"You go into the country far from a city area and people are still traveling with guns. You could look at someone wrong and they would shoot you. You cannot believe the horror. You never know what could happen there, and that's why I feared for her life."

When Tamba arrived in the United States, he could not speak or write English.

"I didn't even know what football was all about," said Hali, who first played football his freshman year in high school. "It seemed too easy. All I wanted to do was reunite my family, and at the time, I didn't even think that football would help me achieve this."

Hali went on to star at Penn State University, and the Chiefs surprised many so-called experts when they made him their number one pick with the 20th overall selection in the draft. The day after he signed his contract, he began working with individuals who could help bring his mother to the United States.

When the Chiefs recorded their first shutout in four years, a 41–0 rout of the San Francisco 49ers, Rachel Hali was in Arrowhead Stadium, sitting a few rows behind the Chiefs bench.

"It was the first time she's ever seen me play," Hali said, sporting an ear-to-ear grin. I can hardly wait to go out and talk to her. She has seen me play on TV—on VHS recordings—but never in person."

Hali's mother arrived in Kansas City the Thursday before the game against the 49ers. She is staying with her son thanks to a one-year visa. A peace agreement ended the conflict in Liberia in 2003, and the last few years have been more peaceful, but economic woes still make it a difficult place to live.

"It was just a great day," Hali said after that win over the 49ers. "She doesn't really understand the game. The family is around her explaining it. I just wanted her to come out here so she can see exactly what's been going on in the United States. Every time I tell her to pray for me so I can have a big game."

She must have said her prayers before the game against the 49ers because her son had one and a half sacks and forced a fumble to star in the defensive-oriented victory.

"It was great, just knowing that it was the first time she had ever been in the stands," Hali said. "I was nervous before the game. She was there, and so was my dad, who was seeing me play in the NFL for the first time."

While he concentrated on improving his skills during the regular season, Hali will now concentrate on making sure his mother can stay in the United States once her visa expires.

In August he flew to New Jersey and passed the test to become a U.S. citizen. He hopes citizenship, along with his stature in the NFL, could make his mother's stay in the United States permanent.

To think, a warlord told eight-year-old Tamba Hali that he had to join the rebel cause or suffer the consequences.

"That seems like such a long, long time ago," Hali said, shaking his head. "Thank goodness those times are behind us. Now, we can concentrate on helping my mother stay in the United States. That was my dream, and I will work until it becomes [reality]."

ALL GOOD THINGS MUST END

The unthinkable happened December 27, 1974.

Hank Stram, the only coach in the history of the Dallas Texans and Kansas City Chiefs, was fired.

He compiled a 124–76–10 record over 15 years, won Super Bowl IV, appeared in the first Super Bowl, and was the winningest coach in the history of the AFL.

"Hank is a very good football coach, his record proves that," team owner Lamar Hunt told the *Topeka State Journal*. "But circumstances and the chemistry of the situation dictate the change."

Len Dawson, the former Chiefs quarterback, said loyalty was one big reason Stram was fired.

"We were 5–9 the year Hank got fired and everyone was getting old at once," Dawson said. "Hank was just so loyal to his guys, the players who had helped him be so successful over the years. And, unfortunately, we all got old about the same time."

Stram was not offered a job in the organization and went on to a short coaching stint at New Orleans. He did not return to Arrowhead Stadium for many years, but was on hand when his name was added to the Chiefs Ring of Fame and Hall of Fame at Arrowhead Stadium in 1987

RETIREMENT HASN'T SLOWED DOWN VERMEIL

The smile is quick and genuine. Dick Vermeil is making the rounds at Arrowhead Stadium, visiting friends from the organization he coached for five years. From receptionists to members of the support staff and janitorial crew, Vermeil has a hug, a greeting, a slap on the back, or a peck on the cheek for everyone. Although he looks years younger than 70, the man who walked away from coaching last season was back to check out his team this past season.

"Oh, gosh, it's great to be back," said Vermeil, who created an offensive juggernaut in Kansas City but still took the Chiefs to only one playoff appearance during his last stop as an NFL coach.

He might be retired from coaching, but he hasn't slowed down. He has worked some ESPN football games and was behind the mic when the Chiefs defeated the Oakland Raiders 20–9 in Week 15. The personable coach gives motivational talks around the country and finds time to do some charity work, fish, and work on his vineyard in the Napa Valley.

Vermeil owns a 126–114 career record in the NFL with stops in Philadelphia (1976–82), St. Louis (1997–99), and Kansas City (2001–05).

Because of his longtime friendship with Chiefs CEO and president Carl Peterson, Vermeil agreed to return to the coaching ranks after leading the Rams to the Super Bowl and then walking away from the game he loves.

"When Carl called and asked me to come to the Chiefs, I did it," Vermeil said, matter of factly. "I wasn't interested in any other job or looking for a coaching job, but Carl and I had been together at UCLA and the Eagles. We were old-time friends. I had broadcast Chiefs games. He'd offered me the job in 1989. It was a good feeling. And I loved [Chiefs owner] Lamar Hunt, so I went."

The Chiefs enjoyed great offensive success under Vermeil as quarterback Trent Green, running back Priest Holmes, and return man Dante Hall turned into Pro Bowl performers. They all credit the coach for much of their success.

"Coach was more like a father to me than a coach," Hall said. "When I was down, he'd pick me up. He and [his wife] Carol mean so much to me. He built up my confidence and was a big reason for my success. He saw something in me that no one else saw. I thanked God every day that he was my coach."

Vermeil coached Green in St. Louis, where an injury turned the starting job over to a guy named Kurt Warner, who led the Rams to a Super Bowl triumph and earned two MVP Awards.

"Coach Vermeil was a special coach," Green said. "If he believes in you, and he certainly did believe in me, he will work with you to make you a better player. He's a wonderful man and a wonderful coach. I owe him a lot."

Vermeil could have coined the phrase *burnout* in regard to coaches. He would sleep in his office at Philadelphia and burn the midnight oil, trying to find an advantage over his opponents. He said his approach to the game changed over the years.

"The first time around, I'd burned the candle at both ends for so long, I just ran out of gas," Vermeil said. "I really needed a break. When I left, I didn't plan to stay out. I planned to take a year off and then come back into coaching. And they hired me to broadcast, and I enjoyed it. It doubled my salary from what they paid me as football coach at that time, because they didn't pay football coaches very much. I went from $75,000 a year to $150,000 a year—that wasn't too bad—and I was only working 18 weeks."

Despite his success in the broadcast booth, he continued to listen to the coaching offers that poured in.

"I had opportunities for interviews every year except one for 14 years," he said. "I finally decided if I felt good about myself, if I felt back in control of my own work habits and passions to win

The high-energy Dick Vermeil retired following the 2005 season after coaching the Chiefs for five years and leaving a lasting imprint on the team.

DID YOU KNOW...

Not only could Marty Schottenheimer not get the Chiefs to the Super Bowl during his 10-year stint as the team's head coach, but he was also a linebacker on the Buffalo Bills team that lost to the Chiefs 31–7 in 1967, keeping Schottenheimer from appearing in the first Super Bowl as a player. He did have a famous roommate with the Bills, former presidential candidate Jack Kemp.

to the point that if I'm ever going to do it, I better do it now. So when the Rams offered me the job, I took it."

He won a Super Bowl in his third year and believed at the time it was the right thing to go out on top. Later he realized that was a mistake.

"We spent three years building something into the best team in football. It was just the wrong decision to leave."

He has since been back to Kansas City to attend the memorial service for Hunt, who lost his battle with cancer in 2006.

"He was a great, great, great, great man," Vermeil said, a misty dampness appearing in his eyes. "He was just an unbelievable human being—kind, warm, considerate, no ego problems. I had a great relationship with him. I strive to be the same kind of man that he was. He touched my life. He really did."

THE BAD

TRAGEDY STRIKES CHIEFS TWICE

The banner headline in *The Denver Post* screamed out the unthinkable: "Chiefs' Mack Lee Hill Dies after Knee Surgery."

Hill was a likeable young running back from Grambling who was an AFL All-Star during his first season in 1963. He rushed for 1,203 yards in two seasons with the Chiefs and was expected to become a star in the fledgling league.

"Mack had it all," quarterback Len Dawson said. "Size, speed, a great personality. His nickname was 'the Truck,' because he just ran over people."

Hill carried the ball 12 times in his final game against the Buffalo Bills. He caught a third-quarter pass from Dawson, was tackled by Harry Jacobs, and fumbled the ball on the play. He injured his knee and had surgery the following Tuesday. Following the surgery his temperature rose to 108 degrees and he went into convulsions. A team of 10 physicians managed to keep him alive for more than an hour using a breaking mask and ice packs in an attempt to bring his body temperature down. But he never regained consciousness. An autopsy showed that he died of a "sudden and massive embolism [a blood clot]."

On the *Buffalo Evening News*, Chiefs team physician Dr. Albert Miller said, "An embolism may be triggered by a fat globule or particle of a blood clot entering the bloodstream and causing circulation blockage at a vital organ."

138

Hill was quite a find for coach Hank Stram and his staff. The 5'11", 235-pound running back from Quincy, Florida, was not considered big enough to play in the AFL and he signed with the Chiefs for $300.

"But he had to make the team to be paid," Stram said. "Mack Lee Hill was a fine gentleman and a great player. He was probably one of the most unselfish players I have ever coached. He was completely dedicated to the team. Football was his life."

To honor Hill, the Chiefs present the Mack Lee Hill Award to their top rookie every season.

"It keeps Mack's name and memory alive," Dawson said, "and that's important, because he was a fine young man."

Hill's death wasn't the first tragedy to strike the team. In 1963, in an exhibition football game against the Oakland Raiders in Wichita, Kansas, former Olympic sprinter Stone Johnson suffered a broken neck. There are few details about Johnson's death. He was a running back with blazing speed who could have teamed with Hill to give the Chiefs a formidable power/speed combo in the backfield. Johnson, who attended Grambling University, died 10 days later. His jersey No. 33 and Hill's No. 36 are both retired.

DELANEY WAS A TRUE HERO

Hero is the most overused word in the English language when it comes to the world of sports. However, when it is used to describe Joe Delaney, it's the perfect adjective for a man who lost his life in an attempt to save three small boys from drowning.

The children were swimming in a rain-swollen lake in Monroe, Louisiana, in June 1983 when Delaney heard their cries for help. Delaney was from nearby Ruston and was visiting Monroe.

"He saw them get into trouble," police officer Marvin Deerman told UPI, "and we think he dived in not knowing how deep the water was and couldn't find the bottom to push up."

AN UNFORGETTABLE TOUCHDOWN

Hall of Fame linebacker Bobby Bell had a dream.

"I always wanted to score a touchdown on special teams," said Bell, the best outside linebacker in the history of professional football. "When I got my chance, I made the most of it."

It was November 27, 1969, and the Chiefs were hosting division rival Denver. The Broncos had mounted a furious fourth-quarter rally and trailed 24–17 with 59 seconds left on the scoreboard clock. Bobby Howfield lined up to kick an onside kick and coach Hank Stram told all his players to fall on the ball and make sure it didn't go back to the Broncos.

"I wasn't even thinking about falling on it," Bell said. "If it came to me, I was taking it back and I was going to do my best to take it back all the way."

Bell got the ball on the far sideline near the Chiefs' 47-yard line and returned it 53 yards for the game-clinching score.

"I picked it up on one bounce and I was gone. No one touched me," Bell cackled. "After that touchdown, I went to the All-Star game and Denver's coaches were coaching the game. They said, 'You dirty dog. Why didn't you just fall on the ball?' That wasn't my style—I wanted to make something happen."

It was 17 years before another Chiefs player returned a kickoff for a touchdown. Boyce Green did it on December 21, 1986, against Pittsburgh.

Delaney, 24, jumped into the pit of water that had been created while construction crews were working on a waterslide. One boy drowned, one managed to get out of the water, and the other was taken to an emergency room.

The accident occurred at a downtown amusement park. The water depth was estimated to be 15 feet. Police divers recovered the body of Delaney and one boy.

Delaney was 5'10" and weighed 184 pounds. Friends said he did not know how to swim, but that that would not have deterred him from trying to help.

"Joe was like a breath of fresh air," Chiefs general manager Jim Schaaf said at the time. "He was so friendly and easygoing and fun to be around. He loved his family, loved life, and loved football. Our hearts go out to his wife and children. He was a special kind of guy."

Delaney was survived by his wife, two daughters, and a son.

Delaney, from Northwestern Louisiana University, was the Chiefs number two draft choice in 1981. He set a club single-season rushing record with 1,121 yards that season and had the longest run (82 yards) and best single game (193 yards) in the NFL. He was the AFC Offensive Rookie of the Year and the UPI Rookie of the Year.

"Joe was one of the most well-liked guys on the team," defensive back Gary Green said. "That [Delaney's death] was a shock. Something like that you can never foresee."

Team president Jack Steadman said, "So many thoughts go through your mind—feelings of sorrow for his wife Carolyn and other loved ones who were closest to him. Their loss is monumental compared to our loss—and we try to keep that in perspective—but we have lost one of the most exciting players in our history."

The Chiefs honored Delaney's memory by wearing a patch that season that featured his No. 37 and a replica of the President's Medal of Freedom that Vice President George Bush presented to the Delaney family in July.

TEAMMATES STUNNED BY SIMMONS'S DEATH

Shock, sadness, and disbelief were some of the feelings expressed by teammates and acquaintances of former Kansas City Chiefs linebacker Wayne Simmons, who died August 23, 2002, in a fiery, single-car wreck on Interstate 70 in the Kansas City suburb of Independence.

"It's such a shock," Chiefs defensive end Eric Hicks told television station KCTV. "Wayne was so energetic and tough. He was a very intense guy and I think one of the best linebackers in the country. He had a good career. It's really sad."

Simmons, 32, a first-round pick in 1993 who won a Super Bowl with the Green Bay Packers, was speeding and weaving his

Wayne Simmons, who was killed in a car accident in 2002, had established himself as one of the top linebackers in the league. Photo courtesy of Getty Images.

green Mercedes through traffic when it went off the roadway at about 2:45 AM, Independence police said.

The car rolled several times, landed in a ditch, and caught fire. Bystanders attempted to pull Simmons from the wreckage but he could not undo his seat belt. Firefighters arrived, put out the fire, and pulled Simmons out. He was transported to the Independence Regional Health Center and was later pronounced dead. He was the sole occupant of the car.

"On behalf of the entire Chiefs organization, our condolences and sympathy go out to the family and friends of Wayne Simmons," Chiefs president Carl Peterson said. "It is a tragedy any time you lose an individual to an early death, particularly in an accident such as this."

"He was a really fun guy to be around," John Schneider (personnel analyst to Packers coach and general manager Mike Sherman) told the Associated Press. "He had an engaging personality, and he was one of those throwback [Oakland] Raider type of characters. Maybe [that hurt him] in his career a little bit, his outspokenness and inability to follow the rules at times."

At Clemson, he had 206 tackles during a stellar four-year career. He anchored the 1990 Clemson unit that led the country in total defense. He had a 73-yard interception return for a touchdown in 1989 to help the Tigers to a 34–23 win over Florida State.

Clemson wide receivers coach Rick Stockstill remembered Simmons as a competitive and unselfish player, "a fun-loving guy off the field, a jokester, but very popular with his teammates."

Simmons graduated with a degree in finance in 1992 and played his final year as a grad student.

"We certainly feel for Wayne's family at this moment and our prayers are with them," Bill D'Andrea, a senior associate athletic director at Clemson who was offensive line coach during Simmons's freshman year in 1989. "He was also an excellent

> **DID YOU KNOW...**
>
> Ed Budde (1963) and his son Brad Budde (1980) are the only father-son duo in the history of the team to be drafted in the first round.

student. He took difficult classes and did not cut any corners academically. He graduated on time with his class."

Green Bay traded Simmons to Kansas City after the sixth game of the 1997 season. The Chiefs cut Simmons the day after the "Monday Night Meltdown," a 30–7 loss to Denver in 1998 in which Simmons and teammate Derrick Thomas were called for a total of five personal fouls on the Broncos' final touchdown drive.

DT

BLOOD CLOT CLAIMS THOMAS'S LIFE

Derrick Thomas's sudden death might have been the biggest, most heartbreaking story to hit the Kansas City area in the past decade. Thomas, a resident of the Kansas City suburb of Independence the past 11 years, died at 10:10 AM EST, February 8, 2000, in Jackson Memorial Hospital in Miami, Florida. Thomas, 33, suffered a brain embolism while being transported to physical therapy. He was being treated for injuries from a car accident on January 23 that left him paralyzed from the chest down.

The former nine-time Pro Bowl selection for the Chiefs was injured on January 23 when the car he was driving flipped on icy Interstate 435, paralyzing him and killing his friend Michael Tellis. Another passenger was wearing a seat belt and was not seriously injured. Thomas and his two companions had been heading to Kansas City International Airport to fly to St. Louis for the NFC title game.

Thomas holds the single-game NFL record for sacks with seven and ranks ninth on the all-time list. His seven sacks against Seattle in 1990 came during a game he had dedicated to his father, an Air Force pilot who was killed in Vietnam.

Thomas didn't just sack quarterbacks, he did his best to sack illiteracy with his acclaimed reading program, the Third and Long Foundation, which has received several national awards. Thomas was a former NFL Man of the Year and one of former President

Derrick Thomas, seen in this 1989 photo, died on February 8, 2000, in a Miami hospital where he was being treated for injuries from a car crash that left him paralyzed from the chest down. Thomas suffered from cardio-respiratory arrest and efforts to resuscitate him failed.

George H.W. Bush's Points of Light, an award which he received from the president in a ceremony in Kansas City.

REMEMBERING A FRIEND

Neil Smith promised himself that this year he wasn't going to cry. Yet the former Pro Bowl defensive end and Blue Springs, Kansas, resident felt the tears stream down his face as the 16 Derrick Thomas Third and Long Foundation scholars were announced to a standing ovation in 2002 at the Kansas City Downtown Marriott Hotel.

"I just knew that Derrick was there, somewhere," Smith said of his former best friend and All-Pro Kansas City Chiefs teammate. "I just started crying. It made me realize all the good that Derrick has done and how much I miss him—how much we all miss him."

Smith and a galaxy of All-Stars from the fields of entertainment and sports converged on Adams Pointe Golf Club in 2002 to participate in the Derrick Thomas Third and Long Foundation Celebrity Golf Classic, which funds the scholarship event. Chiefs Hall of Famers Bobby Bell, Otis Taylor, and Deron Cherry were there; as were former Pro Bowl linebacker Cornelius Bennett and friend Christopher "Kid" Reid (from the Kid 'n Play hip-hop comedy duo). And there, sitting in a corner of the clubhouse, was Edith Morgan, Thomas's mother.

"I feel like every young man in this room is my son," she said. "I told them all that Derrick might be gone, but I'm still here—and I need them now, more than ever."

Thomas founded the Third and Long Foundation, a program motivating inner city youngsters to read.

"When you see those kids walk across the stage," said Reid, who might be remembered for his stovepipe-hat Afro, "you know that Derrick started something special.

"I do a million charity events, but this is one where you can see the good it does. You see those kids get scholarships and know they're going to college and they're going to better themselves. Heck, it might keep them from stealing your car someday."

The mood was upbeat and positive at Adams Pointe as the celebrities and their playing partners stopped off at the clubhouse to chow down on bratwursts and hamburgers.

"You know the real friends are here this year," said Bennett, who anchored the Buffalo Bills' AFC championship squads and played for the Atlanta Falcons and the Indianapolis Colts. "I'm not dissing anyone—I'm just saying that the guys who are here

DID YOU KNOW...

The Chiefs have had just 10 head coaches in the history of the team: Hank Stram, Paul Wiggin, Tom Bettis, Marv Levy, John Mackovic, Frank Gansz, Marty Schottenheimer, Gunther Cunningham, Dick Vermeil, and Herm Edwards.

Derrick Thomas proudly carries the Chiefs flag around Arrowhead Stadium after a big win on December 24, 1995. By beating the Seattle Seahawks 26–3, the Chiefs clinched home-field advantage in the playoffs.

are making sure that something very special never goes away. Derrick's foundation is very special to all of us, and we're going to do anything we can to keep it going."

Betty Brown, Third and Long Foundation president, backed that statement.

"It's easy for guys to fly in for a tournament when they know they're going to be playing with one of their best friends," Brown said. "But now that Derrick is gone, they still come in.

"And fellows like Neil Smith would do anything we ask. He'll call me and say, 'Betty, what do you need? I'll do a commercial. I'll do anything you want.' And that's why we're keeping Derrick's dream alive."

As the bright sunshine glowed on the perfectly manicured course, Thomas's mother whispered, "It seems like it always rained in the past. It rained last year, but Derrick hadn't had the time to make all the proper connections up there in Heaven. Now, he's been there a year, and look at this fine weather. I know he's up there smiling."

THOMAS WILL NEVER BE FORGOTTEN

Over the span of 24 hours, Kansas City Chiefs president and general manager Carl Peterson experienced every emotion known to man. On a Monday afternoon he visited Kansas City Chiefs linebacker Derrick Thomas at Jackson Memorial Hospital in Miami. Thomas, who had suffered a serious spinal injury in a single-car accident nearly three weeks earlier, was sitting in a wheelchair.

"Son, you're mobile," Peterson said.

A grinning Thomas replied, "Father, I am. I have wheels."

Twenty-four hours later, Peterson received a phone call that Thomas had died early in the morning on February 8, 2000.

"Sometimes we're fortunate that an individual can come and transcend your life," Peterson said, choking back emotions. "Derrick Thomas was one of those people."

Peterson said the Chiefs lost more than a great player.

"We lost a great part of this organization," he said. "We also lost a great player and a great person. When I was with Derrick [Monday] he was upbeat, he was positive, he was Derrick."

And Peterson had no explanation for Thomas's sudden and shocking death.

"I don't know if there is any explanation as to what transpired," he said. "I know he had the best medical assistance possible. I know these things do happen, unfortunately, to people who had an accident like Derrick's."

Former Chiefs coach Gunther Cunningham, known as a coach who wears his emotions on his sleeve, managed to fight back the tears as he talked about the player who had been one of his favorites since he was an assistant coach who joined the Chiefs in 1995.

"The last time I talked to him on the telephone [at halftime of the Super Bowl], I wasn't doing real well at the time," Cunningham said. "Derrick said, 'Coach, be strong.' He never told me how strong I had to be. When I heard the news, it was difficult, really difficult."

It was difficult for Chiefs owner Lamar Hunt as well.

"Derrick was an exceptional person. For his family, this is just an impossible void to fill," Hunt told WDAF-TV. "For young people that he helped to learn to read, through his Third and Long Foundation; for the sport; and for Kansas City as a city, and I think for the country, the loss of someone like Derrick Thomas, it's an impossible void to fill. We grieve for his family right now. He will always be in our hearts. It's just a rapid, fast development. It's just a shock."

Cunningham said he talked to about one-third of the team about Thomas's death and said he planned on calling every member of the team throughout the day.

THE BIG CHIEF

One of the first tasks one must deal with when moving a sports franchise is coming up with a new name for the team.

"I'm sure a lot of people think that the Chiefs' name came from the fact that the team was moving to the Midwest and people thought of cowboys and Indians," said Tony DiPardo, who has been the team's bandleader since the move from Dallas in 1963. "Actually, Lamar [Hunt] named the team the Chiefs after the mayor of Kansas City, H. Roe Bartle."

Bartle was a bigger-than-life politician who guaranteed Hunt that the team would triple the number of season tickets sold in Dallas. Bartle was a lawyer, banker, cattleman, college president, executive director of the Boy Scouts of America, and Kansas City's mayor. He earned the nickname "the Chief" while working with Native Americans in Wyoming. He added 3,000 permanent seats to Municipal Stadium and 11,000 portable bleacher seats. He lived up to his promise and they remained good friends until Hunt's death in 1974.

"A lot of people get a lot of credit for things in the Kansas City organization, and rightfully so," he continued. "But I don't think that whatever you say about Derrick Thomas, he gets enough credit for filling Arrowhead week after week. I think I can speak from all sides—as an assistant coach, a head coach, and an opponent—how frightened we were to come to Arrowhead and try to block him.

"But then, he'd come across the field after the game with a smile on his face, not because the Chiefs won, but because that's what he was.

"And that's how I will remember him."

WHAT MIGHT HAVE BEEN

PLAYING FOR MORE THAN PRIDE

As hard as he tried, Len Dawson couldn't get the lyrics to *The Mickey Mouse Club* out of his mind. It had nothing to do with the cute little cartoon character who was created by Walt Disney; it had more to do with a comment by *Sports Illustrated* writer Tex Maule, who called the American Football League a "Mickey Mouse League" in a conversation following a Green Bay Packers game.

Dawson's American Football League champion Kansas City Chiefs were set to battle Vince Lombardi's National Football League Green Bay Packers in the first AFL-NFL world Championship Game.

Chiefs owner Lamar Hunt called it the "Super Bowl," after the hard, rubber Super Ball his children played with, but the name didn't stick until three years later.

"All the talk surrounding the game centered around the Packers and how they were the superior team and the superior league," Dawson said. "We weren't just playing for our team and our city, we were playing for an entire league."

And that *Mickey Mouse Club* theme kept wafting through Dawson's mind.

"They were the older, more experienced league," Dawson said, "but we had some pretty good teams in the AFL and we had some pretty darned good players play in that game."

Four Chiefs who played in the game—Dawson, linebackers Bobby Bell and Willie Lanier, and defensive lineman Buck Buchanan—and coach Hank Stram all found their way to the Football Hall of Fame.

"There was a war of words leading up to that game," Stram said. "We were all eager to get it settled on the field."

Stram issued a gag order for his team: no bad-mouthing the Packers or the NFL.

"Hank didn't want any trouble," said the colorful Fred "the Hammer" Williamson, a defensive back who went on to enjoy a successful career in Hollywood, where he appeared in several movies, including *M*A*S*H* and *I'm Gonna Git You Sucka*. "I wanted to get the attention focused on me, to take the pressure off the other guys."

Williamson talked about how he was going to lay the hammer down on the Packers, which provided good bulletin board material for Lombardi's 13-point favorites.

"I don't think Fred did us a favor by saying all the things he did," Dawson said, "but at least he was confident going into the game. Looking back at it, we were extremely confident going into the Championship Game against the Bills [a 31–3 AFL championship victory that led to the Super Bowl], but we weren't that confident going into the game against the Packers.

"We were a young team. I was one of the oldest guys on the team, and we had the talent to play with them, but on that sunny day in Los Angeles, they were the better team."

The first Super Bowl wasn't quite the extravaganza it is today. There were only 338 print media and 262 electronic media

DID YOU KNOW...

Michael Jackson and his brothers kicked off their Victory Tour with three sold-out performances on July 6, 7, and 8, 1984, at Arrowhead Stadium. The Arrowhead maintenance crew had to tear out a wall so all of Jackson's sound equipment could reach the field. The wall was later rebuilt.

Len Dawson tries to scramble out of the pocket in the first Super Bowl, in which the NFL's Packers proved to be too much for the Chiefs in a 35–10 loss in January 1967. Photo courtesy of Bettmann/Corbis.

credentials issued. There were more than 13,000 credentials to media issued from all over the globe for Super Bowl XLI. A "spaceman" wearing a jet pack—similar to one that was featured in a James Bond film—thrilled the crowd of 61,000 fans, who somehow seemed lost in the 90,000-seat L.A. Coliseum. Tickets were $10 and $12. Face value tickets to the 2007 Super Bowl were $600 and $700 and many were sold via ticket booking agencies for five to 10 times that amount.

"Lamar always thought the Super Bowl was going to be big," Dawson said, "but I don't think anyone thought it would be what it is today. It's almost as if the game can get lost in everything that goes on during the week before the game. All the Hall of Fame guys are down there, there are more parties than you can count, and look at the entertainment. We had a guy fly around the stadium and a couple of bands."

Prince, the Rolling Stones, and Paul McCartney performed at the past three Super Bowls, 2005, '06, and '07, and Janet Jackson's revealing performance in 2004 will be remembered long after the winner of this year's event is forgotten.

Lombardi would have nothing to do with all the hype surrounding the first Super Bowl. He took his team 90 miles up the coast of California and practiced away from all the scrutiny.

"Our plan was to get inside [defensive back Willie] Mitchell," Lombardi said back then. "They were daring us to pass. That stacked defense worked well against the run, but we felt like we could get inside Mitchell and he wouldn't have any help."

Lombardi had the perfect quarterback to execute that plan in Bart Starr, an accurate passer who never put up huge numbers because he was usually asked to hand the ball off to Jim Taylor and Paul Hornung.

"Our game plan was perfect," Starr said on a visit to a Kansas City charity event. "We knew exactly what we wanted to do, and they had a hard time stopping it."

One player emerged as a hero for the Packers, and he happened to have been out on the town the night before the big game because he didn't think he would see any action. His name is Max McGee, and he was an 11-year veteran backup to wide receiver Boyd Dowler.

McGee, who legend has it returned to his hotel room at 7:00 AM the day of the Super Bowl, caught seven passes for 138 yards and two touchdowns. He scored the first touchdown in Super Bowl history when he reached out with one arm and somehow managed to snag a pass that had been tipped by Mitchell. He rumbled 37 yards for the score and the Packers led 7–0.

The play didn't rattle the Chiefs as Dawson hit Otis Taylor on a 31-yard pass play that put the ball on the Packers' 7-yard line. On the next play running backs Curtis McClinton and Bert Coan were both standing alone in the end zone; Dawson fired a perfect strike to McClinton to knot the score.

Jim Taylor then scored on a 14-yard run for the Packers and the Chiefs got a 31-yard field goal from Mike Mercer to make the halftime score 14–10 in favor of the Packers.

"We were confident at the half," Bell said. "We all felt like we had played well, stuck to the game plan, and that we could come out and make something big happen in the second half."

Something big did happen in the second half, and to this day it causes nightmares for Dawson. Facing an all-out Packers blitz, Dawson looked for Fred Arbanas on the right side of the field. His off-balance pass was tipped and intercepted by Willie Wood on the Chiefs' 45-yard line. He returned it to the Chiefs' 5 and Elijah Pitts scored on the next play. Suddenly the Packers had momentum and a 21–10 lead.

"If there is one play I could have back in my entire career," Dawson said, "it would be that one pass."

Although he never pointed an accusing finger at Dawson, even Stram said, "I would like to think that one play doesn't make a difference in an entire game, but in that case it did. Our personality changed; we diverted from our game plan."

Offensive lineman Dave Hill recalls, "After they got the big lead, they started coming after Lenny. They were throwing everything at us, and we didn't do a very good job of stopping them."

Dawson and backup Pete Beathard were sacked five times in the second half. McGee caught a 13-yard touchdown pass, Pitts scored on a one-yard run, and the Packers proved the world right by claiming a convincing victory over the Chiefs.

"You have to give Green Bay a lot of credit," said former Chiefs general manager Jack Steadman. "They had everything to lose and we had everything to gain. Lombardi was getting a lot of pressure."

DID YOU KNOW...

Three members of the Chiefs—defensive back Fred "the Hammer" Williamson, defensive lineman Buck Buchanan, and return man Nolan "Super Gnat" Smith—appeared in the legendary film M*A*S*H. They were among the ringers who played a football game against another surgical unit.

Arbanas, who still calls Kansas City home, wonders what might have happened if the ball had not been tipped.

"I was open and could have had some running room," the All-Time AFL tight end said. "They caught us off guard with that blitz."

Dawson agrees.

"They hadn't blitzed the entire game. I made the biggest mistake a quarterback can make—just take a loss and don't turn the ball over. I've replayed that pass over and over and over again in my mind."

If you're wondering whatever happened to the bold Fred "the Hammer" Williamson, he was knocked unconscious by Packers running back Donny Anderson early in the game and never returned to action.

After the game, Lombardi received the championship trophy—which now bears his name—and said, "Kansas City has a good team. But it doesn't compare with some of the top teams in the NFL."

The Chiefs bristled at those comments and vowed to return to Super Bowl action to prove they could compete with the elite teams of the NFL.

CHIEFS RECEIVE A LUMP OF COAL THIS CHRISTMAS DAY

During the glory years of the Kansas City Chiefs there were three certainties in life: death, taxes, and Jan Stenerud connecting on game-winning field goals.

"If the game came down to Jan, you knew we had a win," quarterback Dawson said. "He was automatic."

Perhaps that's why there is still an air of disbelief concerning the Chiefs 27–24 double-overtime Christmas Day loss back in 1971. While the Chiefs were hoping for frigid temperatures, it was an unusually warm day when the Miami Dolphins paid a visit to play in the final game at Municipal Stadium.

The winner of this game would go on to the AFC title game, and the Chiefs were heavily favored against a Miami team that was just beginning to earn its place among the elite squads in the NFL.

The Chiefs had dominated most of the game, but the scrappy Dolphins came back and knotted the score at 24–24 with less than two minutes to play when Bob Griese hit Marv Fleming on a five-yard touchdown pass.

"We knew there was plenty of time left to do something in regulation," Dawson said, "and we didn't panic. We just went to business."

Ed Podolak, who will forever be remembered for his Christmas Day performance in this game, took the kickoff 78 yards, and for a few moments, it appeared he might go all the way. But Miami's Curtis Johnson knocked him out of bounds to keep the Dolphins' slim hopes alive.

"Right then, it didn't look very good," Miami coach Don Shula said, "because they had Stenerud."

The Saturday before the big matchup between the Chiefs and the Dolphins, Stenerud had been named to the Pro Bowl team, even though Yepremian led the league in scoring. Now, the future Hall of Famer was pacing the sideline, waiting for his chance to kick the Chiefs into the AFC title game. The Chiefs ran two plays to give Stenerud the perfect spot on the field to kick a 32-yard chip shot.

"All Hank [Stram] wanted to do," Dawson said, "was give Jan the perfect opportunity to win the game."

With 35 seconds left in the game, the Chiefs called a timeout and Stenerud trotted out on the field. He had been the hero of Super Bowl IV two seasons earlier, giving the Chiefs an early 9–0 lead in the game with three field goals, including a then–Super Bowl record 48-yarder.

The native of Norway, who came to the United States on a ski jumping scholarship, never appeared flustered or nervous. He took his place a few steps behind Dawson, and Bobby Bell snapped the ball.

"The snap was good, the hold was good," Dawson said, "and Jan got all of it."

As the hushed crowd of 45,822 watched the flight of the ball, a sudden gasp sucked the wind out of Municipal Stadium and gave new life to the Dolphins.

The ball sailed inches outside of the right upright.

"It's unbearable, totally unbearable," Stenerud told a group of reporters in the locker room after the game. "I have no idea what I am going to do now. I feel like hiding. I don't feel like ever playing football again."

That miss set the stage for what would become the longest game in the history of the NFL. After the miss Stenerud walked back to the sideline, was briefly consoled by Stram, and prayed that his team would find a way to give him another opportunity.

"There was no question in my mind I was going to make that field goal," Stenerud told Dick Connor in the book *Kansas City Chiefs*. "And I still don't know to this day how I missed it. There was hardly any wind and the turf, at that spot, was pretty good. It wasn't in the middle and it wasn't on a hashmark.

"It was kind of in-between, so I think that the only thing I could have done wrong was line it up a little wrong. You know, soccer-style kickers have a little angle. I hit it well—it was straight, high, and nice—and since it was only three or four inches outside the right upright, it may have been a mental mistake, where I lined it up wrong."

The Chiefs got the ball first in the overtime period and quickly moved into field-goal range. Stenerud made a silent promise to himself that if given a second chance, he would send his teammates and the raucous fans home happy. Stenerud lined up for a 42-yard attempt, but the ball never got near the goal posts; Miami linebacker Nick Buoniconti broke through the line and blocked it.

"Nick was a great player," Dawson said, "and great players make great plays."

Yepremian missed from 52 yards out, and the game went into the fifth quarter.

"We were all tired, dog tired," Dawson said, "but this game meant so much to each team. It was like two heavyweights slugging it out. Neither team was going to throw in the towel."

The Chiefs offense could do nothing and punted the ball to the Dolphins, who started what would be the final series of the game on their own 30-yard line.

"I CAN'T QUIT SMILING"

"Have you ever had a smile on your face for 24 straight hours?" asked Kansas City Chiefs return specialist Dante Hall. "I can't quit smiling."

The reason for the ear-to-ear grin was simple. Hall was the first member of the Kansas City Chiefs to ever appear on the *Late Show with David Letterman*.

Hall and his mother, Carolyn, were taken by limo to the Ed Sullivan Theater in New York, where Hall appeared on the same program with bombshell actress and former Playmate Pamela Anderson.

"The *Late Show* and Pam all on the same night," Hall said. "No wonder I'm grinning."

That season Hall helped the Chiefs get off to an 8–0 start with an NFL record–tying four kick returns for touchdowns. *Sports Illustrated* called him the NFL's Most Valuable Player at the midway point of the season and Hall wasn't just the toast of Kansas City, he was the toast of the Big Apple.

"It was incredible," Hall said of his late-night appearance. "Something I will never forget."

Miami quarterback Bob Griese was aware that the Chiefs linebackers had shut down Larry Csonka and Jim Kiick on any attempt to run the ball outside.

"We had a lot of plays we liked to run," Griese said back then, "and in the huddle I was going over them in my mind. There was one play we hadn't called, and I thought it would work. Csonka liked it and they had been killing us on their sweeps."

Griese called the "Csonka Special," a misdirection play that started to the right but featured a quick cutback to the left. He was finally tackled at the Chiefs' 36-yard line.

Three plays later and the ball was on the 30. Shula sent Yepremian onto the field, and he kicked the game-winning 37-yard field goal.

"When I saw [teammate Karl] Noonan signal that Garo's field goal was good," Griese said, "I broke out laughing. I just laughed, I was so tired."

More than three decades after that loss, Dawson admits that, "There isn't a day that goes by that I don't think about that game. So many people point an accusing finger at Jan, but it shouldn't have come down to his field goal. In fact, the game wouldn't even have gone into overtime if it hadn't been for a mix-up earlier in the game."

The Chiefs took a quick 10–0 lead at the start of the game, but the Dolphins always found a way to come back and knot the score. Tied at 10–10 in the second quarter, the Chiefs' offense stalled on the Dolphins' 22-yard line, and Stenerud came out to attempt what appeared to be a field goal.

"The center [Bell] was supposed to snap the ball to me, not Lenny," Stenerud said. "I was going to run around the right end. Miami was really overloaded to that side, and this was the perfect situation to run."

Dawson agreed.

"The play was sent in from the sideline and we were all ready for it," Dawson said. "At least, I thought we were ready. When Bobby snapped the ball, it came right to me. I didn't know if he hadn't heard what I said or if he thought that something was wrong with the play, but it came back to me like a normal kick. I yelled out, 'Kick it!' and he did. And he missed.

"As we were walking back to the sidelines, I asked Bobby what had happened and he said he looked at Jan and thought he'd missed the call. I guess Jan sold it so well, he faked out Bobby. I know it would have been a big first down—no telling how far Jan could have run with the ball. He was a big, athletic guy—a ski jumper—and it was the perfect call at the perfect time.

"It's funny. Most fans don't even know about that play. They just remember Jan missing at the end of the fourth quarter, and that's just not fair to Jan."

THE GAME OF HIS LIFE

Christmas Day 1971 and Ed Podolak: in Kansas City Chiefs folklore, the two are inseparable. Podolak became a star for the ages in the final game ever played at Municipal Stadium back in 1971 on a balmy Christmas Day in a contest that featured two of the best teams in the NFL.

He accounted for a total of 350 all-purpose yards, scored two touchdowns, and kept the Chiefs in the two-overtime slugfest that Miami eventually won on a 37-yard field goal 82 minutes and 40 seconds after the opening kickoff.

"The Dolphins were just becoming one of the better teams in the league," Chiefs quarterback Dawson said, "and they would go undefeated the next year and win the Super Bowl.

"But in 1971 I thought we had the best team in football. For the first time in many years, everyone was healthy. We had Otis Taylor and Eddie [Podolak] on offense and that great defense with Buck [Buchanan], Willie [Lanier], and Bobby [Bell] and great special teams players in Jan [Stenerud] and Jerrel [Wilson].

"We were all very confident that we would win that game against the Dolphins, and we should have. I still think about that and I think about the game Eddie played. I don't know if I've ever seen a better performance. We all left everything out on the field that day—especially Ed Podolak."

Podolak was nothing more than a solid NFL running back—until that Christmas Day performance turned him into a rock star.

"I might be in an airport or a restaurant and someone will recognize me and ask about that Christmas Day game," said Podolak, who still looks as if he could carry the ball 25 times and score a touchdown or two. "It's amazing that people remember that game after all these years."

What's even more amazing is that even though the game was sold out, it was not televised in Kansas City because of NFL blackout rules. Those Chiefs fans who didn't have a ticket had to drive as far away as Clinton, Missouri (where the author watched the game on his grandparents' television), to catch the action.

Podolak finished the game with eight receptions for 110 yards and a touchdown, 17 carries for 85 yards and a touchdown, three kickoff returns for 155 yards, and a one-yard punt return.

"It was the greatest single-game performance I ever saw," Chiefs coach Hank Stram said, "especially when you consider the circumstances. You know the term, 'playing your guts out?' Well,

DID YOU KNOW...

Tight end Fred Arbanas lost the sight in his eye following an assailant's attack in 1964, but he came back to play through the 1970 season. He was named the AFL's All-Time top tight end by the Pro Football Hall of Fame.

that's what Eddie and his teammates did that day. They played their guts out."

The Chiefs were holding on to a 24–17 lead when Miami quarterback Bob Griese hit Marv Fleming with a game-tying five-yard pass with one minute and 36 seconds left in the game. Podolak brought the sold-out crowd to its feet when he returned the kickoff 78 yards.

"I thought I was gone," he said, as he met with other members of that team at a Chiefs Reunion Game at Arrowhead Stadium. "Curtis Johnson had the angle on me and ran me down. I must have watched that film 100 times, wondering if there was anything I could do, any way I could get away from him, and there wasn't. At the time I thought it was good enough because Jan could come in and kick the game-winning field goal."

Stenerud came in and missed a 31-yard field goal.

"If Jan makes that field goal, the game is over and we go to the AFC Championship Game," Podolak said. "But if the game doesn't go six quarters and have all that drama, no one probably remembers my name."

He grinned, and added, "But I'd trade my one day in the spotlight for another chance at a [Super Bowl] ring. I was a rookie on that 1969 team [that won Super Bowl IV] and we had more talent, more depth, and fewer injuries on the 1971 team. I think we could have gone on and won another Super Bowl, but I guess we'll never really know, will we?"

THE UGLY

THE HALL OF SHAME
Public enemy number one: Lin Elliott

Jan Stenerud was the first pure place-kicker to be inducted into the Football Hall of Fame in Canton, Ohio. He played for the Chiefs from 1967–1979 and he still owns or shares nine team records, including 16 consecutive games scoring a field goal.

He was replaced by Nick Lowery, a journeyman kicker who tried and failed to make 10 different NFL teams and vowed Kansas City would be his final stop.

Then head coach Marv Levy thought the young man with the strong leg would be the perfect replacement for the aging Stenerud, and Lowery finally won a job.

He held on to that job until 1994, when the number one all-time member of the Kansas City Chiefs Hall of Shame arrived on the scene.

His name was Lin Elliott.

"You don't want to say that name too loudly in Kansas City," quipped Len Dawson, "because he still invokes a lot of bitter memories."

Elliott had been dumped by the Dallas Cowboys for whiffing on too many important field-goal attempts; the Chiefs believed a new change of scenery would do him some good. Little did they know what awaited Elliott and Chiefs fans, who were so desperate for a postseason victory.

Chiefs kicker Lin Elliott misses a 42-yard field-goal attempt that would have tied the game in the final minutes of the AFC divisional playoff game against the Indianapolis Colts on January 7, 1996, in Kansas City.

Elliott slumped badly during the end of a memorable 13–3 1995 regular season. In a game against the Raiders he missed a field goal and two extra points, but those are little more than blips on the radar screen compared to the bombshell he would drop at Arrowhead Stadium as the Chiefs prepared to host the Indianapolis Colts.

The Chiefs had a Super Bowl defense, and an offense that had managed to put enough points on the scoreboard to secure home-field advantage throughout the playoffs. All the Chiefs had to do was beat a wild-card team from Indianapolis—a team that played its home games in a dome, a team that had no respect in the league and a journeyman quarterback.

At least they didn't have Elliott.

He missed field goals from the 35-yard line, the 39, and a possible game-tying attempt from 42 yards late in the game. Colts kicker Cary Blanchard hit a 30-yard attempt in the third quarter that turned out to be the game winner in a stunning 10–7 loss that Chiefs fans are still mourning.

"I tried my best," said Elliot in a locker room where many of his teammates lay on the floor, still in their uniforms, trying to deal with what had just happened.

That missed attempt against the Colts was Elliott's last field-goal attempt in the NFL.

THE QUARTERBACKS

Bill Kenney

There is nothing quite as difficult in the world of professional sports as following a legend. Ask Kevin Seitzer, who followed George Brett at third base in Kansas City, or Bill Kenney, who was asked to take over the quarterback reigns a few years after fans watched Len Dawson's Hall of Fame career.

As the next-to-the-last player taken in the 1978 draft, Kenney certainly didn't come into the NFL with any great aspirations or dreams of grandeur.

With the tragic death of Joe Delaney, who drowned trying to save two boys who had fallen into a Louisiana pond, the Chiefs had to find someone to put the ball in the air in 1983, and Kenney responded with a 4,000-yard season. Despite his success, the team was just 6–10 and never in contention in the AFC West the entire season.

It would be unfair to place all the blame on Kenney, who was 46–51 as a starting quarterback. Stuck with the Chiefs' porous offensive line, he spent more time on his back than a mattress salesman.

As Kenney's All-Pro wide receiver teammate Carlos Carson said, "I don't care who you are, it's tough to throw a pass when you're lying on your back."

Kenney holds one team record he would gladly relinquish: most times sacked in the history of the Chiefs (195). He was the starter when the team lost the most games in a row in team history (nine in 1987) and didn't win a road game in 1985.

Any of the team's success during Kenney's tenure came from a defense that was led by nose tackle Bill Maas, a secondary that ranked among the best in the league, and a group of special-teams players that made coach Frank Gansz (who would go on to become a disastrous head coach) the most talked about assistant in the league.

Todd Blackledge

Quick, name the most disappointing number one draft pick in the history of the Chiefs. Come on, time is running out. If you said offensive lineman Trezelle Jenkins, you are close, but incorrect. Jenkins is certainly the most embarrassing and talked-about pick of the Carl Peterson era as he quickly proved that he couldn't block a Pop Warner player on crutches. But the man the Chiefs selected with the seventh overall pick in the 1983 draft still casts a shadow over an organization that has never developed a quality quarterback.

Hall of Famer Len Dawson sat the bench for years in the NFL before joining the then Dallas Texans and going on to enjoy a Hall of Fame career with the Chiefs. The team got Joe Montana a

The heralded quarterback class of 1983 poses in the year 2000, in the order in which they were drafted: from left, Hall of Famer John Elway (1), Todd Blackledge (7), Hall of Famer Jim Kelly (14), Super Bowl quarterback Tony Eason (15), two-time Pro Bowler Ken O'Brien (24), and Hall of Famer and multiple record holder Dan Marino (27). Photo courtesy of Bettmann/Corbis.

AN UNTIMELY POTTY BREAK

Former Dallas Texans and Kansas City Chiefs owner Lamar Hunt missed the most famous coin flip in the history of the AFL.

The Texans were tied with the Houston Oilers in the AFL Championship Game when Dallas captain Abner Haynes won the toss and inadvertently said his team wanted to kick into the wind, rather than have it at the team's back.

"Lamar Jr. was six and he had to do what most six-year-olds have to do—use the bathroom," the elder Hunt said, "so I missed the flip and all the confusion."

Quarterback Len Dawson still recalls the flip and Haynes's infamous call.

"The wind was blowing 100 miles per hour and Hank wanted to have the wind at our back to start overtime. Abner said we wanted to kick to the clock, which meant the wind would be at the back of the Oilers. But it didn't matter. Bill Hull intercepted a pass and we eventually won in the second overtime on a Tommy Booker 25-yard field goal."

After he and Lamar Jr. returned from the restroom, the founder of the AFL saw the rest of the two overtime periods.

"I remember Bill Hull's interception and Jack Spikes's long run that set up Tommy Booker's field goal," Hunt said. "It was a raucous postgame locker room. I'll never forget that."

few years past his prime. Steve DeBerg was a gutsy quarterback who didn't have enough talent around him to make a difference. And you'll read about Steve Bono and Elvis Grbac later in this chapter. Draft picks David Jaynes, Steve Fuller, Mike Elkins, and Matt Blundin could appear in a police lineup and no one would recall that they were members of the Chiefs. But they pale in comparison to Todd Blackledge, the pride of Penn State, who was supposed to be the savior when he was drafted in 1983.

Instead, he threw more interceptions (32) than touchdowns (26), lost his starting job to Bill Kennedy and watched the Chiefs struggle through a five-year stretch where their record was 34–45. He faded from the playing field to the broadcast booth, where he provides color commentary for NCAA football games.

Steve Bono

When gold was discovered in the hills of California, the cry across the United States was "Go West, young man! Go West!" When the Chiefs were in desperate need of a starting quarterback, CEO and President Carl Peterson did the same thing—he went west.

For two glorious years, former San Francisco 49ers legend Joe Montana played quarterback for the Chiefs, leading them to the 1993 AFC Championship Game, only to be knocked unconscious in a loss at Buffalo. Wanting to be able to play with his kids and not be confined to an easy chair the rest of his life, Montana retired following the 1994 season and Peterson again went in search of gold. While he struck it rich the first time, this trip west just provided a payload of fool's gold.

The Chiefs brought Steve Bono into town and he quickly made enemies with all the Kansas City barbeque fans by proclaiming there wasn't a restaurant in town that could compare to even the worst joint in the Bay Area.

With Bono at the helm, the Chiefs enjoyed a 13–3 season in which the defense ranked among the best in the league. Derrick Thomas and Neil Smith made sure that the quarterback with the hair that never moved didn't blow the team's chances for home-field advantage throughout the playoffs.

When they received the first-round bye and followed that with a home game against the lowly Indianapolis Colts, it appeared the path to a Super Bowl would go through the heart of the Midwest. The Chiefs were hoping for freezing temperatures, and that's what they got as they played host to a team that played its home games in a dome. Starting in his first postseason game, Bono was dreadful. He threw three interceptions and led the team to just one touchdown.

However, the Chiefs did get close enough to the end zone for two failed Lin Elliott field-goal attempts. Late in the game coach Marty Schottenheimer pulled Bono in favor of backup Rich Gannon, a fan favorite and the quarterback favored by his teammates.

Gannon led the team deep into Colts territory, setting up the potential game-tying field goal from 42 yards out. Elliott missed again, and the Colts claimed a 10–7 victory. After the game Bono was asked about his performance and he said, "I felt pretty good out there today." He was 11 of 25 for 122 yards.

Ouch!

Elvis Grbac

This Elvis was anything but a king, and Chiefs fans applauded when he left the building. While Todd Blackledge was the worst number one draft pick in team history, the worst decision of the coaching and front-office staff was made when Rich Gannon was let go and the team threw mad money at Grbac, yet another former 49ers quarterback.

Gannon went on to win an MVP Award and led the Raiders to the Super Bowl. Grbac became the whiniest, most disliked quarterback in team history.

After a home loss to Pittsburgh in 1998, he topped Bono's comment about Kansas City restaurants with the most inflammatory remark in team history. When asked about the team's play, he said, "I can't throw the ball and catch it too."

He looked like a chicken with its head cut off in a 1997 playoff loss to Denver when he ran around the field, cupped his hands to the side of his helmet and pleaded for help in the most disturbing and unsuccessful two-minute drill in team history.

Grbac had no idea how to handle that pressure and his final pass was well out of reach of wide receiver Lake Dawson in the end zone. Instead of spending more time in Kansas City in the off-season, the man who wore a Cleveland Indians baseball cap thought he could improve his luck by changing from No. 11 to No. 18.

Wrong!

In his last season with the Chiefs, he asked to sit out a game against the winless Chargers because of a bruised finger. A few years earlier, Steve DeBerg played quarterback in a game in which he broke his thumb and the bone broke through the skin. DeBerg had a huge bandage put on the thumb and returned to action. The rallying cry that season was "Win one for the thumb!"

Elvis Grbac walks off the field as the Chiefs prepare to punt in a 1997 game against the New Orleans Saints.

The Chargers won that game as Grbac watched from the bench. It was San Diego's only win of the season.

Perhaps Grbac's "crowning moment" came on a Monday night loss to New England in which Grbac again self-destructed—only this time it happened in front of a national television audience.

Down by four with two minutes to play, Grbac threw a fourth-down pass to tight end Tony Gonzalez, who was double covered on the 4-yard line. Gonzalez caught the ball but was tackled, and the game came to an end. When asked why he didn't throw into the end zone to give his team a chance to win, Grbac could not come up with an answer.

That was his final season with the Chiefs. To prove that he hadn't learned much from his disastrous stay in Kansas City, he signed with the world champion Baltimore Ravens and promised to take the team "to a new level."

Elvis has left the building—thank goodness.

THE JAIL BIRDS
Bam Morris

Bam Morris should have been best known for being the leading rusher in the Pittsburgh Steelers' 1996 Super Bowl loss to Dallas. Instead, he was known as the guy police found with six pounds of marijuana in the trunk of his car. He told the police it was his personal stash and was placed on probation.

Proving you can play in the league no matter what skeletons hang in your closet, Morris signed with Baltimore. He failed a drug test and was sentenced to 10 years in prison. A plea deal was struck and he served 89 days.

Morris promised to be a good boy and joined the Chicago Bears. He couldn't get on the field in Chicago, so the Chiefs gave him a chance to clean up his act.

All he did was clean up selling drugs and stolen vehicles as he was a part of a nationwide theft and drug ring that included his teammate Tamarick Vanover. He and Vanover are such bad apples, they have their own chapters in the ugly history of the teams.

Tamarick Vanover

Tamarick Vanover was a former Canadian Football League product who became the team's star return man. His overtime punt return for a touchdown against the San Diego Chargers in 1995 led to one of the most thrilling moments in Arrowhead Stadium history.

But his off-field shenanigans soon overshadowed everything he did on the football field. He was part of a group that stole luxury automobiles in and around North Carolina, brought them back to Missouri, where they were retitled and sold outside of the state. It was one of the largest theft rings in the nation.

Because he cooperated with the government investigation and pointed the finger at those other members of the group, Vanover received a light sentence. He attempted to play for former Chiefs coach Marty Schottenheimer in San Diego, but failed to make the grade. In 2006, he signed on with tiny Lake

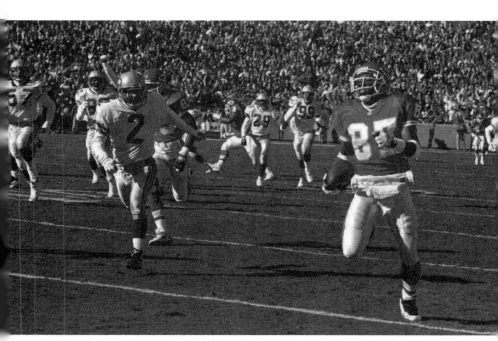

Tamarick Vanover was better at outrunning opposing defenses than he was the law, as shown here during an 89-yard touchdown return of the opening kickoff against the Seattle Seahawks in December 1995.

City Christian Academy in Lake City, Florida, to be its head football coach and athletics director. Perhaps he is one former NFL bad boy who finally has his life headed in the right direction.

Andre "Brock Middlebrook" Rison

Andre Rison first made headlines in the NFL with his memorable "Bad Moon Rison" nickname. It was a fitting moniker for one of the game's top receivers and most flamboyant members. After all, how many guys can say his pop star singing sweetie burned down his mansion?

Rison earned a Super Bowl ring in 1996 with the Green Bay Packers and even caught a touchdown in the game. For once, he was getting attention for what he did on the field, not off. When he signed with the Chiefs in 1997, he was a model citizen and solid wide receiver, catching 72 passes for 1,092 yards and hosting youth groups as part of his charitable activities.

Had he become a new man, given a second chance at life in the NFL?

No.

Rison, who had given himself the nickname "Spiderman" earned a new nickname after an arrest in a bar at the Chiefs' preseason training home in River Falls, Wisconsin. When the arresting officer was filling out his report on the incident, he asked Rison his name, he replied, "Brock Middlebrook."

It got plenty of chuckles from Chiefs fans and his teammates.

No one was laughing in 1990 when Brock was arrested outside of the Have a Nice Day Café in Westport. Brock and teammate Lonnie Johnson were held out of the Chiefs' next game "for conduct unbecoming a player." When Gunther Cunningham took over as head coach, he made the team stay at a hotel in Kansas City the night before a home game to eliminate such incidents.

In 2000, Brock was charged with felony theft in Olathe, Kansas. He posted $2,000 bond on a felony charge of stealing musical equipment and was then released. The Johnson County sheriff's department said the equipment had been rented, but never returned. The Chiefs released the man with the many nicknames in 2001.

THE REST OF THE WORST

Victor Riley

Victor Riley, a 1998 first round draft pick, saved his hardest hit for his wife and child in 2001. The big offensive lineman was suspended for one game during the 2001 campaign for violating the NFL's personal conduct policy.

Angry at his wife, Riley rammed her vehicle with his SUV. The couple's infant child was in the vehicle alongside his mommy while daddy was "doing his thing."

Riley was charged with felony counts of aggravated assault and criminal damage to property, misdemeanor counts of child endangerment, and leaving the scene of an accident. In 2006 he became a backup lineman with the Houston Texans.

Mark McMillan and Carlton Gray

The Chiefs brought 5'7", 150-pound Mark McMillan into camp to play nickel back in 1997. He was small, but he made the cut and should have been a fan favorite. But every time the diminutive back made a play, he would strike a Mighty Mouse pose, taunt the receiver, and basically act like an idiot. He was an embarrassment to the team, the NFL, and the famous cartoon character. The Chiefs tried him at cornerback in 1998, but that experiment failed miserably, so he was finally released and replaced by Carlton Gray.

Gray signed a huge contract after starting in Seattle, but will forever be known in Kansas City for one play—and it didn't even take place during a regular-season game. The Chiefs were scrimmaging the New Orleans Saints in River Falls when several players got into an argument. While a Saints player was under a pile of Chiefs and his own teammates, Gray sucker punched him.

The moment was caught on television and replayed over and over and over again. The fans hated Gray, his teammates had no respect for him, and he rarely saw the playing field again, sitting out 12 of 16 regular-season games in his final year in Kansas City.

Dan Williams

Dan Williams joined the Chiefs in 1997 and made an immediate impact. After playing four years in Denver, where he spent more

DID YOU KNOW...

Tom Bettis served as an interim coach in 1977 following the firing of Paul Wiggin (11–24). Bettis owns a 1–6 career record as a head coach in the NFL.

time in the training room than the playing field, it appeared the massive nose tackle had finally found a football home.

He started six games and had 10.5 sacks. Williams had signed a one-year deal and was after some big bucks in 1998, but the Chiefs wanted to make sure he wasn't a one-hit wonder. Williams and the Chiefs could not come to an agreement, so Williams sat out the entire season.

Facing a problem that has been an Achilles' heel for the Chiefs since Peterson's arrival in 1989, the team was desperate for a nose tackle. They signed Williams to a four-year deal with a $7.8-million signing bonus. He never regained the form, or desire, he had shown his first year and coach Dick Vermeil cut him in 2001.

Ryan Sims and Junior Siavii

If you think the Chiefs have had problems drafting a quarterback, look at their last two defensive tackles. The team traded up in 2002 to get Ryan Sims, who coach Dick Vermeil called "fat and out of shape." Sims has produced the type of lackluster stats that would find most players on the unemployment line: 59 games, 64 tackles, 10 assisted tackles, five sacks, and one interception. That's barely over a tackle a game and his sack total is embarrassing. But because he is a former first-round pick, he's still wearing red and gold.

The lack of an inside push on the defensive line has been a major setback for a team that is so desperate to replenish its defensive line that it again drafted a big man to plug the middle of the line. In 2004, the Chiefs traded down to get Junior Siavii with the 36th overall pick in the draft. Siavii is following in the footsteps of Sims, as he had one sack and one fumble recovery in two years. Siavii even got into a fight with in a Minneapolis hotel bar in

2005 and had to be subdued by the police. When they wrestled the big man to the ground, which probably wasn't much of a problem, they had to place a spit hood over his face to keep him from ...well... spitting on them. Siavii was not a favorite of Vermeil's and he was finally cut in 2006 when Herm Edwards took over the team. Edwards proved he was a man of his word when he said, "By the end of the day, if your uniform isn't dirty, you're not going to play for me." Guess he meant covered in dirt, not spit.

Dale Carter

Dale Carter was one of the finest defensive backs in the history of the Chiefs. He was also one of the most troublesome. He had several brushes with the law during his career from 1992 to 1998, including an arrest following a shootout outside of a Kansas City nightclub in 1993. Police reports claim Carter and two passengers were in a truck about 1:30 AM when they were fired upon. One of the men in the truck returned fire and no one was injured.

After signing with Denver as a free agent, he was suspended from the league for violation of its substance abuse policy.

Bennie Thompson

One of the top special-teams players in Chiefs history, Bennie Thompson was a Plan B free-agent signee who will forever be remembered for an incident that took place after making a fierce tackle on a kickoff return.

"I don't remember what year it happened," said Dawson."But Bennie makes the tackle, then gets down on all fours and acts like he's urinating on the ball. It's just like what you would see a dog do. If you're talking about the good, the bad, and the ugly, that would have to fit under two categories—bad and ugly!"

WHAT WERE THEY THINKING?

WHAT WENT SO TERRIBLY WRONG?

Bam Morris and Tamarick Vanover were the poster children for all that was wrong with professional football. Morris, a bruising running back who was supposed to energize a once-proud backfield in the late 1990s, and Vanover, an electric return man whose game-winning punt and kickoff returns for touchdowns made him an instant Kansas City folk hero, both wound up spending time behind bars for their roles in a variety of criminal activities.

Morris, who faced sentencing guidelines calling for a five-year prison term, was sentenced to two years and six months in jail in 2001 for his role in conspiracies to sell marijuana and launder drug money.

At his sentencing, the Associated Press reports that Morris said, "First of all, I want to tell my family and friends that I'm sorry. I was wrong. I made a mistake. I ask the court to be lenient."

He received a lighter sentence because he helped federal prosecutors with ongoing criminal cases. Morris, who also played for the Baltimore Ravens and the Pittsburgh Steelers, was also fined $10,000 and must spend five years under supervised release after serving his sentence. Vanover was sentenced to two months in a federal jail, another two months of home detention, and three years of federal supervision after that. He was also ordered to pay a $10,000 fine and make $6,241 in restitution to an insurance company for its losses related to the vehicle theft. Like Morris,

DID YOU KNOW...

In 1995, the west end zone of Arrowhead Stadium was nicknamed "Hallelujah Corner" when three games resulted in victories following returns for touchdowns. James Hasty picked off a Jeff Hostetler pass and returned it for a touchdown to give the Chiefs a 23–17 overtime win; Tamarick Vanover returned a punt 86 yards to give the Chiefs a 29–23 overtime win over San Diego on *Monday Night Football*; Vanover also returned a kickoff 89 yards to that same corner of the end zone to lead the Chiefs to a 26–3 win over Seattle.

Vanover received a lighter sentence for his help in the investigation of other related cases.

The sentencing was part of an ongoing federal investigation of nationwide drug dealing and car theft. The AP reports the drug ring smuggled more than 200 pounds of cocaine to Kansas City each month, and the car-theft ring sold stolen luxury cars around the country.

Vanover asked for forgiveness at his sentencing, saying, "First of all, giving honor to Christ, who is the head of my life, to my family, the judge, and the community, I would like to say I'm truly sorry for my shortcomings.

"I realize that I have made a big mistake that has nearly cost me my family and my childhood dream. However, there have been some positives that have come out of the situation, including a better bond between my family and myself, rejoining the church, and recommitting myself to Christ, because I realize without him, nothing would be possible. My character and the people I socialize with have also changed for the best."

Assistant U.S. Attorney Mike Oliver asked that the minimum penalty guideline of five years be cut in half because of Morris's cooperation with the government.

Morris, a former Texas Tech star who led the Steelers to the Super Bowl in 1996 and was that game's leading rusher, pleaded guilty last August 4 to two of four counts of a federal indictment. He admitted attempting to distribute more than 220 pounds of

ARROWHEAD STADIUM FIRSTS

- First game: September 17, 1972, a 20–10 loss to the Miami Dolphins
- First play: Jan Stenerud kickoff for a touchback
- First play from scrimmage: Miami running back Mercury Morris's 11-yard run
- First Chiefs tackle: Safety Mike Sensibaugh tackled Morris
- First pass play: Bob Griese's incomplete pass
- First Chiefs play from scrimmage: Wendell Hayes's one-yard run
- First completed pass: Len Dawson to Hayes for an 18-yard gain
- First fumble: Chiefs running back Ed Podolak
- First touchdown: Griese to Marlin Briscoe for 14 yards
- First rushing touchdown: Larry Csonka, who was also the first back to rush for 100 yards (118 yards on 21 carries)
- First Chiefs points: 40-yard Stenerud field goal
- First Chiefs touchdown: Dawson four-yard pass to tight end Willie Frazier
- First Chiefs win: November 5, 1972, a 27–14 over the Oakland Raiders

marijuana in the Kansas City area between January 1, 1998, and May 10, 2000. Court records show that money for the deal came from Vanover.

Morris, who was already on probation for a 1996 marijuana conviction in Texas, retired from the Chiefs shortly before his indictment on the federal charges was made public. After being cut by the Steelers following the Super Bowl, Morris signed with the Ravens, for whom he rushed for more than 700 yards the next two seasons. But each year he was suspended by the NFL for violating the league's substance abuse policy, and the Ravens released him in January 1998.

Morris's probation was revoked, and he was sentenced in 1998 to 10 years in prison, serving only 89 days after his attorney arranged a plea bargain. He was signed and cut by the Chicago Bears, for whom he never played, and Kansas City picked him up in October 1998.

Shortly after he agreed to cooperate with authorities, the Chiefs cut Vanover, who plead guilty to aiding and assisting in the sale of a Ford Expedition that was stolen from Kansas City and sold in Tallahassee, Florida.

Vanover agreed to tell all he knew about what was described as a "large-scale, organized, and structured" drug ring that obtained marijuana and cocaine from sources in Mexico, California, and Texas for distribution in Kansas and Missouri.

Chiefs president Carl Peterson issued a statement that said Vanover was no longer a member of the Chiefs.

"Last month I indicated that I would continue to weigh the facts as they became known to me as a federal case involving Tamarick Vanover continued to evolve," the statement read. "In light of information contained in a federal affidavit that has come to my attention today relative to admitted activities involving Vanover, I have found it necessary to terminate him as a member of the Kansas City Chiefs."

Information provided to authorities by Vanover led to convictions of at least six other people, including his former teammate Morris, a federal prosecutor said.

Vanover first came to the attention of federal authorities in the spring of 1999 as they investigated the Kansas City end of a cocaine trafficking ring based in Fresno, California.

On January 25 prosecutors charged Vanover's friend and personal assistant, Gregory E. Burns, with cocaine trafficking. The same day Vanover agreed to cooperate with investigators and began four days of interviews with federal agents.

Records show Vanover gave Burns $8,000 to buy cocaine and Morris $40,000 to buy marijuana. Burns later pleaded guilty to unrelated drug trafficking charges.

WARFIELD'S "DUMB, DUMB, DUMB" MOVE

If Eric Warfield could turn back the hands of time, he would do it. He is the first to admit that he made a mistake—a "dumb, dumb, dumb" mistake. He feels embarrassed and he knows he let an

Eric Warfield had a better handle on the face mask of Tennessee Titans wide receiver Chris Sanders than he did with his DUI record, where he was a three-time offender.

entire city and all his teammates down when he was suspended by the league for the first four games of the 2005 season. He knows he should have called a cab. When he was stopped by police his blood alcohol level was .189. "I could have jumped in a cab," Warfield said. "I could have ridden with somebody. It was just dumb, dumb, dumb. Why did I do it? I have been asking myself that same question."

Because Warfield was suspended the first month of the 2005 campaign, the Chiefs relegated him to the sideline, where he stood with all the reserves.

Once one of the premier defensive backs for the Chiefs, he spent most of his afternoons standing and watching the starters go through their drills.

"That's hard," the veteran cornerback said, "really hard. I'm watching everyone go right on by me."

Warfield is a three-time DUI offender (none of the incidents involved an accident). After the police stopped him the third time, he eventually spent 10 days in jail and 80 days under house arrest. Shortly before training camp it was announced that Warfield would miss the first four games of the season.

"I may not be on the field, but I will be there for my teammates," Warfield said. "I'll cheer them on, I'll work hard, and hope that I can come back and contribute. But I know there are no guarantees."

Coach Dick Vermeil made that evident when he said, "He understands that he's not going to just walk back into his job," Vermeil said. "From here on out, he has to do everything right on and off the field. He is providing other people the chance to prove what they can do."

Warfield knows it will be no problem staying in shape, but he wonders about being in "football shape."

"There's a difference," said Warfield, who could not use the team facilities during the suspension. "I need to be in a position where I can work out, do the things I'd be doing if I wasn't suspended."

He knows he made a mistake, a huge mistake. But he is also thankful deep down inside that he never did anyone harm while driving under the influence.

"As bad as things seem, they could have been worse. What if I would have been involved in a wreck with a family? I couldn't live with myself if that happened."

The 2005 season was Warfield's last in Kansas City.

DID YOU KNOW...

Running back Abner Haynes was the AFL's first Most Valuable Player in 1960. In three seasons in Dallas he scored 44 touchdowns.

MONDAY NIGHT MELTDOWN

THOMAS APOLOGIZES FOR ROLE IN MONDAY NIGHT MELTDOWN

For the past decade, Derrick Thomas has been the symbol of defensive excellence for the Kansas City Chiefs. However, a two-minute span in the fourth quarter of an embarrassing 30–7 *Monday Night Football* loss to the Denver Broncos back in 1989 might wipe aside all the good things Thomas has done and leave a stain on the perennial All-Pro's career as a member of the Chiefs. He was called for three personal fouls in the Broncos' final touchdown drive and was suspended by the Chiefs for one week without pay. Fellow linebacker Wayne Simmons, who was also whistled for a personal foul in the touchdown drive, was waived by the Chiefs.

"I'm embarrassed," Chiefs coach Marty Schottenheimer said before a two-hour closed-door meeting with Thomas. "It's one thing to play the game and lose. There is no shame in losing. But to do what a couple of our players did is inexcusable."

Thomas was banned from Arrowhead for one week. He was not permitted to use any of the Chiefs' facilities or attend team meetings or practices. A repentant Thomas met with the media and offered a heartfelt apology.

"I want to apologize to my mother, who attended the game, and my grandmother, who watched on television, to Marty and to Mr. [Lamar] Hunt [the Chiefs owner] for my conduct Monday night," Thomas said, choosing to talk from the heart rather than read from a prepared statement.

Denver's Terrell Davis breaks through the Kansas City defense seemingly at will during a particularly embarrassing loss for the Chiefs under the spotlight of a national *Monday Night Football* audience. Photo courtesy of Getty Images.

"What happened was not characteristic of my game. I allowed a situation to get out of hand. I apologize to my teammates for letting the situation get out of hand and hinder our chances of winning the game.

"Those actions will never occur again. I like to think that I am one of the individuals on the team people like to look up to. From here on out, I will conduct myself in a manner that is positive all the time."

He went on to apologize to youngsters who admire him as a player and the young people who are a part of his Third and Long reading foundation.

He said he definitely felt like the punishment fit his actions.

"I will not appeal the Chiefs' decision," he said. "I have been here 10 years and this is the most difficult thing I've ever had to deal with. To not be able to play, to not be able to help my team win—that is very difficult. I want to compete."

Thomas said there were many contributing factors to his actions, in which he grabbed the face mask of Denver tight end Shannon Sharpe on two different occasions. He said he watched Sharpe use a cutback block on Simmons and that he was enraged by the move.

"Shannon tries to intimidate, to antagonize," Thomas said, "but that's no excuse for my actions."

He said he hoped the suspension and being benched because of his inability to help the defense stop the running game do not leave a permanent stain on his career.

RAIDER HATERS

An all-time record crowd of 82,094 watched the Chiefs beat the hated Oakland Raiders 27–14 Chiefs' November 5, 1972, to claim the first-ever win at Arrowhead Stadium.

The game marked the first installment of the legendary rivals that dated back to the days of the AFL. Len Dawson threw three touchdown passes, Ed Podolak ran for 115 yards, and Jan Stenerud kicked two field goals and was perfect on three extra-point attempts.

"There was just something different when it came to playing the Raiders," Dawson said. "They really didn't like us and we didn't like them. It was fitting that the first win in a new stadium would be against Oakland."

One of the few bright spots of the Marv Levy coaching era came October 11, 1981, when the then second-largest crowd in Arrowhead history (76,543) watched the Chiefs blank the Raiders 27–0.

Oakland could manage just 79 yards on the ground and 129 in the air, and much-maligned quarterback Bill Kenney passed for 287 yards and two touchdowns.

"I'm a man," he said. "I'm human. I made a decision and I know it was the wrong decision. This has been a very frustrating season. I just want to get back and help this team play."

SMITH WATCHES AS CHIEFS SELF-DESTRUCT

Neil Smith watched something he couldn't believe—the complete meltdown of his former team.

"I saw it, but I couldn't believe it," Smith said after his Denver Broncos embarrassed the Chiefs 30–7 before a nationally televised *Monday Night Football* audience at Arrowhead Stadium in 1998.

"I don't know how such a good team, a team that was 13–3 last year and a team that has basically the same players, could go downhill so fast."

When asked if he felt any sympathy for his former teammates, the Broncos All-Pro defensive end smiled a sad smile and said, "I want to feel sorry for them, but I can't. I just can't."

Smith, who still lives in the Kansas City suburb of Blue Springs, didn't leave on the best terms before the start of the 1997 season. He said the Chiefs told him his best days were behind him. That didn't sit too well with the five-time Pro Bowl performer. But he kept his mouth shut, signed with the Broncos, and came away from the 1997 season with the Super Bowl ring that had eluded him during all the years he spent in Kansas City.

"I didn't want to leave Kansas City," Smith said, "but now that I'm in Denver, man, I never knew what I was missing. This is a team. I mean, we care about each other. Our coach cares about us. What I saw, I wonder if any of those guys [on the Chiefs] care about each other.

"I looked over and saw the Chiefs, but I felt like I was looking at the old Oakland Raiders, the dirty bunch of Raiders who were penalized all the time and were so easy to beat.

"I think the Chiefs and Raiders have traded places this year. That last drive is all you need to look at to see what I'm talking about."

The last drive he was referring to was an 80-yard touchdown drive by the Broncos that was fueled by five Kansas City personal foul penalties—three by Smith's best friend on the Chiefs, Derrick Thomas, and one each by Chester McGlockton and Wayne Simmons. "I've never seen anything like it," Smith said. "We couldn't believe what we were seeing."

Neither could Chiefs coach Marty Schottenheimer, who watched his team allow an amazing 62 yards and five first downs on penalties.

"We lost our poise," said Schottenheimer, who slumped in a chair as he discussed the low point of his 10-year coaching career in Kansas City. "We have no self-restraint. Quite frankly, some put their personal interests ahead of this football team. The frustrations of this season and the outcome of the game contributed to this. But there is no excuse. None. Zero."

DID YOU KNOW...

The artificial turf at Arrowhead Stadium was replaced by grass in 1994.

Sparked by Kansas City's disregard for the rules, the Broncos drove to the Chiefs' 2-yard line. Derek Loville capped the drive with a two-yard run.

When asked if this was the toughest stretch of his coaching career, the weary Schottenheimer said, "Absolutely. We need more discipline. I told them that in the locker room."

Another former Chief who signed a free-agent deal with Denver, tackle Keith Traylor, was another witness to the *Monday Night Football* assault who couldn't believe what he was seeing.

"When I was a free agent and didn't know if I'd sign with a team, I was concerned," said Traylor, a two-year starter for the Broncos. "But Denver gave me the opportunity and I am so happy to be away from Kansas City. I don't think I could take being on the other side tonight. That team has so many problems. I wouldn't even know where to start."

KICKED IN THE GUT BY SOME COLTS

BLACK SUNDAY

Neil Smith hadn't attempted to take off his uniform as he sat in front of his locker, staring into it as if he were seeking answers to a question that would haunt him for years and years to come.

Derrick Thomas lay sprawled out in front of his locker, tears streaming down his face.

Several teammates attempted to console Thomas, who refused to talk—the pain was simply too intense.

In the background, a crashing noise could be heard as someone muttered that a member of the Kansas City Chiefs had just attempted to rip the training room door off its hinges.

And there, in front of his locker, sat Lin Elliott, looking like a man who had just lost the ticket to a million-dollar lottery prize.

He had just missed three field goals, including a 42-yard effort that would have tied the game in the fourth quarter, and the lowly Indianapolis Colts now owned a stunning 10–7 victory over the highly favored Chiefs.

The year was 1995 and All-Pros Smith and Thomas had paved the way to a 13–3 regular season that saw the Chiefs gain the home-field advantage throughout the playoffs.

"This is our year," said Thomas, the enthusiastic and some-times outspoken linebacker who brought the art of sacking the quarterback to new heights during his reign in the 1990s, before the game.

DID YOU KNOW...

Hall of Fame linebacker Bobby Bell was an all-state quarterback at Cleveland High School in Shelby, North Carolina. Bell won the Outland Trophy while starring on the defensive side of the ball at the University of Minnesota.

"I don't see how any team can stop us, the way we're playing defense. We have the bye [week] and we're playing at home. Doesn't get much better than that."

Not only were the Chiefs playing at home, but they were also playing host to the lowly Indianapolis Colts, a wild-card playoff entry coming from the cozy confines of a home dome.

"They won't know what hit 'em when they come to Kansas City and have to play outside," Thomas said. "I hope there's a foot of snow on the ground."

There was no snow, but it was 8 degrees with a windchill that dipped to 2 degrees. And Arrowhead Stadium was rocking, filled with more than 77,594 die-hard fans who would have traded their grandmas for a playoff victory.

The Colts had a journeyman quarterback named Jim Harbaugh who proclaimed after the win, "We're ragamuffins. I was running out to the middle of the field, jumping around and acting like an idiot."

Football oftentimes brings out the little boy in professional athletes, and Harbaugh wasn't about to apologize for his actions.

"I felt pretty good," he said.

With Tony Siragusa, their best defensive player, in his hotel with the flu and star running back Marshall Faulk sidelined with an injury, the Colts still somehow found a way to beat the Chiefs.

The Colts seemed to savor their underdog role. They were a dome team coming to Arrowhead Stadium, where the Chiefs were 8–0 during the regular season, and yet they didn't bat an eye.

"We've had to go out to prove we are a contending team and quiet all those people who ask, 'Who the heck are the Colts?'"

said Ashley Ambrose, who had one of Indianapolis' three interceptions. "We don't need superstars."

The Colts used second-half interceptions by Ambrose, Quentin Coryatt, and Eugene Daniel to keep the Chiefs off the scoreboard. Ambrose set up Cary Blanchard's decisive kick, while Coryatt's was wasted when Blanchard was short from 49 yards.

When Elliott failed from 42 yards with 37 seconds left, the celebration began for the Colts.

"Nobody expected us to win," said safety Jason Belser, whose father Ceasar played for the Chiefs. "Nobody expected this but the fans we had up in the rafters and the guys in this locker room. We believe in the people we're playing with. When we play as a team, we can play with anybody."

While the Colts were talking about team unity, the Chiefs locker room was as divided as anytime in the team's history. The defense had been sensational all season, while the offense had struggled. Many players, including the key members of the defense, wanted gritty Rich Gannon to take over as quarterback. Coach Marty Schottenheimer put Gannon in the game with four minutes and 12 seconds left in the fourth quarter, hoping to spark the lifeless offense.

Starting at his own 18-yard line, Gannon got them as far as the Indianapolis 36, then ran for 14 yards on third-and-eight. But the offense sputtered and Elliott trotted out on the field. When his 42-yard attempted kick sailed left, Arrowhead Stadium was as quiet as a morgue.

"It's so disappointing to have the best record in football at 13–3 and take a week off and then play like we did today," Gannon said.

A few lockers away from Gannon, Elliott answered one wave of reporters' questions after another.

"I tried my hardest," said Elliott, who also missed from 35 yards in the first half and 39 yards in the fourth quarter. "Maybe I'm not good enough, but I tried. Maybe I was not good enough today, but it's good enough for me as a person to know that I tried. This is not going to be the best night of my life. We're not going any further, and that hurts."

NOT EVEN A PRIEST COULD SAVE THE CHIEFS

Priest Holmes should have been on top of the world. The best running back in the NFL broke the Kansas City Chiefs single-game rushing record by running over, around, and through the Indianapolis Colts for 176 yards and two touchdowns. But all he had to show for his effort was the bitter disappointment that came from a 38–31 loss in the second round of the 2004 playoffs. It the third time since 1995 that the Chiefs had come into the playoffs with a 13–3 record only to lose a game at home.

"This feels a little bit worse, deep inside," Holmes said when asked about the loss. "We know we were playing to win. But actually we needed to be able to play perfect to get past the Colts. They did a wonderful job as far as what they did on offense. Definitely their defense stepped up when they needed to. We didn't play a perfect game but we were playing to win, and with that it wasn't enough today."

The Colts scored every time they had the ball with the exception of two meaningless drives at the end of the half and the end of the game. The one time the Chiefs stuffed Peyton Manning and co., double fouls wiped out the play and the Colts went on to score the eventual game-winning touchdown.

"I think they allowed for us to run the ball and make the catch," Holmes said. "The one thing that they made sure they would do is wait for us to make a mistake. And definitely we made a number of mistakes, myself with a fumble, and not scoring when we needed to do so, especially that first drive and not getting seven points. They did a good job being in place and making sure they could stop us."

Despite the embarrassing performance by the defense, Trent Green and the Chiefs offense put 31 points on the scoreboard. But they could not match the perfection of the Colts offense. Eddie Kennison dropped a first-down reception, Marc Boerigter dropped a touchdown pass, and Johnnie Morton had two passes to the numbers carom off his chest.

"We felt like we had to play perfect considering the situation we were under," Holmes said. "We had to make sure that we could come back being 7 under and then 10 points and then 14 points.

Priest Holmes runs 60 yards for a touchdown against the Washington Redskins in an October 2005 game.

That's a situation where you can't make mistakes. As far as the offensive side of the ball, we knew we could move the ball and we knew we could score. But like I said, we didn't play a perfect game."

Return man Dante Hall turned in a near-perfect performance, returning a kickoff for a 92-yard touchdown that Holmes hoped might turn the game around.

"The momentum had swung, and our '12th man,' the crowd, could feel it too," Holmes said. "Dante had done what he's always done, and that's being spectacular and stepping up in big games. For him to go and take the ball down and score, we really felt that the defense would go back out there with the crowd cheering them on and [get it done].

"We thought it would be too loud for Peyton to make the right calls or audibles, but once again, all the signals he was using even got me confused, and I was on the bench."

Holmes completed a storybook season that happened to have a nightmarish final chapter.

He broke both the single-season touchdown (27) and single-season rushing touchdown (26) marks and proved to everyone that he was fully recovered from his off-season hip surgery.

As he watched the clock tick off the final seconds of the 2003–04 season, he was battling his emotions.

"It feels really bad," he said. "You know that the game is coming closer and closer to an end. And when you have to be on the bench as an offense watching the clock go down, it's very frustrating. It's something that will linger for a long time until we're able to get back and ready."

THE PLAYOFFS ARE A DIFFERENT BEAST

Kansas City Chiefs coach Herm Edwards saw something in his players' eyes when they walked off the field following a season-ending 23–8 playoff loss to the Indianapolis Colts on January 6, 2007.

And he didn't like it.

"I looked in those players' eyes as they came off that field and it looked a lot different than the regular season," the first-year head coach said at Arrowhead Stadium following the last game of the 2006 season. "It's called the playoffs. That's what it is. It's called not being in a playoff game on the road since 1994. We had starters who had been in playoff games, but never on the road. That's a scary thought. Well, they learned something."

So did their coach, whose biggest challenge has been developing a team that can be playoff-ready every season.

"When we get back in the playoffs and have to go on the road, they'll learn how to handle it. When we played that same team [while Edwards was the head coach of the New York Jets] the first time Tony [Dungy] took them on the road, we beat them 41–0 in

Herm Edwards and his Chiefs, who ended the 2006 season with a
disappointing road playoff loss to the eventual Super Bowl champion
Indianapolis Colts, pledge to keep the team competitive in the years to come.

the playoffs. The same quarterback, that same offense, got beat
41–0 on the road. Okay, that's one game."

But that final disappointing loss was one playoff game that
Chiefs fans had been anticipating since 2003—the last time a
Chiefs squad reached postseason play.

"We're making one big deal about one game," Edwards said,
following a 9–8 season. "You know what would have happened if
we had scored 35 points and the defense had given 40? It would
have been the same old defense. I know how to play the game. I
was born at night, but I wasn't born last night. I know how it
works. It's a process."

That process is ongoing at Arrowhead Stadium, where
Edwards, president and CEO Carl Peterson, and the Chiefs coaching and scouting staffs are evaluating the team and preparing for
the 2007 season.

"I took over [this team] a year ago," Edwards said. "I'm evaluating the whole thing. Was it a successful season? It was a good season. It's never acceptable unless you win the championship. Maybe those standards are a little bit high."

Edwards had to deal with the loss of quarterback Trent Green due to a concussion, the retirement of left tackle Willie Roaf, and an offense that had to get accustomed to a new coordinator in Mike Solari.

"When you look at our season, it's a season of difficulty at times," the coach said. "Starting off the season at 0–2, then we regrouped pretty well as a football team and as a staff and got on a pretty good run, winning seven out of nine. Then we lost three in a row, and that to me was the critical part of our season.

"When you lose three in a row in the month of December, that doesn't add up for you. But we found our way out of it and won two in a row at the end and got in the playoffs. Obviously, we didn't play like we anticipated against a team that's been in there a lot the last five years.

"Anytime you can go to the playoffs, it's an experience your team has to get through. This team will learn from that. That's the thing about playoff experience. You have to learn. I thought we had a lot of young players who actually played pretty well in the game."

But all anyone remembers about that loss is a first half in which the Chiefs could not manage a single first down.

"I thought it was a game where we couldn't move the ball offensively," Edwards said. "But that was that game. The week before, we played against a pretty good defense at home and scored 35 points. When you look at what happened to us all

---

DID YOU KNOW...

Greg Kinnear portrayed former Chiefs coach Dick Vermeil when he was coaching the Philadelphia Eagles, in the movie *Invincible*. The film is the story of former player Vince Papale, who earned a spot on the 1976 team as a walk-on during open tryouts.

season, I think it was a learning process for all of us. For me, it was a time to learn about my team and for my coaching staff to learn about me. That's how you've got to start. I was hired a year ago... I've learned a lot about this organization. I've been gone [from Kansas City] for 10 years.

"With that being said, the next thing is to look at the future and where we're headed. We've got some tough decisions to make. There's no doubt about it. We'll make those in a manner that's best for the football team. It's never personal. That's what we have to do at this point in time. We won't have that in a day or two. We have time. I know you people don't have time; you want your answers today for the questions you're going to ask tomorrow. But it doesn't work that way in life or football. It's a process, and we're going through a process of everything we do."

When Edwards arrived in New York, he took over the reins of a veteran team much like the Chiefs.

"It's kind of funny because when I went up there to New York, I had to make a tough decision," he said. "It was a veteran team. Do I keep these guys? I felt obligated to the veteran players that we could get this team to the playoffs, and we did. We did, and everyone said it was Bill's [Parcells] team and that was fine.

"The next year we had another pretty good draft and we won the division. We get into the playoffs again. But that third year, the wheels fell off the wagon. We were an older team and we dismantled it. We actually started seven new guys on defense.

"We lost the quarterback that year and were 6–10. The quarterback got well, we retooled it, and missed a 42-yard field goal to go to the AFC Championship Game. We spun it around and the last year we lost 13 starters including the quarterback. But those players they have there now have been in a lot of playoff games. Rightly so, that's what we talked about up there.

"Is it my team after this year? Yeah, it's my team the first year. I just believe when you become the head coach, they become your guys. I don't care who drafted them. You just want them to buy into what you're trying to do. I think these guys did that. Was it different for them? Yeah, some things were different. Did I ask certain players to do something different? Yeah. Did I do some

A NEW PAIGE IN THE RECORD BOOK

Not much good happened to the Kansas City Chiefs in the 1980s. But on one sunny, glorious Sunday afternoon at Arrowhead Stadium, Stephone Paige wrote his own special chapter in the NFL record book.

When then all-time Chiefs receptions leader Henry Marshall was sidelined with a shoulder injury, a young kid from Fresno State—whose first name was often mispronounced and misspelled—hauled in eight passes for 309 yards.

"That was my day," Paige said at a Chiefs reunion gathering. "Everything went my way that day—everything."

In the first quarter he caught 56-yard and 51-yard passes from starter Todd Blackledge. Paige missed most of the second quarter with bruised ribs and Blackledge suffered a dislocated thumb. Yet with Bill Kenney as quarterback, Paige went on to enjoy the game of a lifetime.

"They just kept covering me with single coverage," Paige said.

Paige's NFL record lasted for four years, until Willie Anderson of the Rams caught passes totaling 336 yards against the Saints in 1989.

things differently in how we play the game? Yeah. So it was a learning process, and for the coaches too. This year will be a lot easier in a lot of areas. When I ask the coaches and players, they can anticipate."

There has been so much talk about Green, who is coming off a first year in which he struggled with an injury and his performance on the field.

Edwards said he is sticking with the veteran quarterback for now.

When asked if Green was his starter, Edwards said, "Yeah, all the starters are the starters right now."

Could that change?

"Oh, yeah, a lot of things could change. But right now, as we start the 2007 season, he's the starter. There will be competition, and that's the whole key. It doesn't matter if a guy's the starter on paper or not. What you want to do on your football team—and we did a pretty good job of it this year—you create competition at the positions. That's what we have to do through the whole roster."

Edwards came to town with a reputation for getting his teams in the playoffs and emphasizing defense. He didn't sugarcoat his opinion on the up-and-down offensive performance of his 2006 Chiefs.

"Am I disappointed? Yeah," he said. "Are the players disappointed? Yeah. Will we do some things offensively different? Yeah. We'll do some things different. I think people think I came here and changed this offense. I really didn't. I changed how we think but I didn't change plays. I didn't do that. I didn't change the terminology. I changed coordinators, and I think he's going to be a heck of a coordinator. I think he went through a growing process and I think he'll be a lot better next season.

"But will I do some things different on offense? Absolutely. I have to. Have to do it that way. I have to feel comfortable with the players we have and what direction we want to head in. But that doesn't mean we're going to run the option. It doesn't mean we're not going to throw a pass."

CHIEFS TRIVIA

RETIRED CHIEFS JERSEY NUMBERS

3—Jan Stenerud (1967–79). The first pure place-kicker in the Pro Football Hall of Fame, Stenerud played 19 years in the NFL, including 13 with the Chiefs.

16—Len Dawson (1962–75). A Hall of Famer and Kansas City icon, Dawson was the MVP of Super Bowl IV which he led the Chiefs to a 23–7 victory over the Minnesota Vikings.

28—Abner Haynes (1960–64). The first star running back of the AFL's Dallas Texans, Haynes led the team in rushing for four years and was AFL Player of the Year in 1960.

33—Stone Johnson (1963). A quarterback from Grambling who was a sprinter at the 1960 Olympics, Johnson suffered a broken vertebra in his neck in a preseason game and died 10 days later.

36—Mack Lee Hill (1964–65). An All-Star as a rookie, Hill suffered a knee injury in a 1965 game and died on the operating table two days later.

63—Willie Lanier (1967–77). A member of the NFL's 75th Anniversary All-Time Team, the middle linebacker was the second Chiefs player inducted into the Hall of Fame.

78—Bobby Bell (1963–74). Called by many the greatest outside linebacker of all time, Bell was the first Chiefs player inducted into the Hall of Fame. He did not miss a single game during his 12-year career.

86—Buck Buchanan (1963–75). A number one draft pick from Grambling, Buchanan anchored the Chiefs defensive line during the glory years and earned a spot in the Hall of Fame.

CHASING THAT PLAYOFF DREAM

As incredible as it might seem, the Chiefs have not won a playoff game since 1993. Here is a year-by-year summary of the team's playoff woes.

1994: The Chiefs get the final wild-card berth but head down to Miami and lose to the Dolphins 27–17.

1995: The Chiefs are *Sports Illustrated* cover boys. But Lin Elliott misses three field goals, and after gaining home-field advantage, the Chiefs lose their first playoff game 10–7.

1996: The Chiefs lose three games to end the season and end any hopes of returning to the playoffs.

1997: The Chiefs are 13–3 and earn the home-field advantage once again, but this time lose to the Broncos 14–10.

1998: The season that will be remembered for two things: the embarrassing Monday night meltdown loss to Denver and Marty Schottenheimer's last (and only losing) season in Kansas City.

1999: The Chiefs needed to win the finale at Oakland to have any hope of making the playoffs; instead, they lost on an overtime field goal by Joe Nedney in Gunther Cunningham's first year as head coach.

2000: Cunningham is fired following a 7–9 campaign that leaves fans and the Chiefs' front office restless and looking for a new direction.

2001: The Chiefs welcome Dick Vermeil, but he fails to work magic that helped him create a Super Bowl champion in St. Louis, and the team finishes with a disappointing 6–10 record.

2002: The Chiefs head to Oakland to play the last game of the season and dream about a return to the playoffs only to lose 24–0 and finish at 8–8 and miss postseason action for the fifth year in a row.

2003: Vermeil creates an offensive juggernaut as his team starts out 9–0 and finishes 13–3, but loses a heartbreaking 38–31 playoff game to Peyton Manning and the Indianapolis Colts in a contest that featured no defense whatsoever.

2004: Chiefs follow up the 13–3 campaign with a miserable 7–9 mark.

2005: A home loss to Philadelphia comes back to haunt the Chiefs as they fail to make the playoffs despite a 10–6 record.

2006: The moon, stars, and planets are aligned in the proper fashion on the final day of the season and the 9–7 Chiefs manage to return to the playoffs under first-year head coach Herm Edwards, but look lackluster in yet another postseason loss to the Colts.

ABOUT THE AUTHOR

Bill Althaus is an award-winning sports writer and columnist for *The Examiner* in Independence, Missouri. He is only the second member of the Kansas City metro area to win the prestigious Gordon Docking Award, which was presented at the 2006 Simone Awards. The award designates Althaus as the Kansas City Media Personality of the Year. His work has been honored by United Press International, the Associated Press, and the Missouri Press Association.

Althaus won the Missouri Press Association's Better Newspaper Contest for a feature he wrote on a three-sport high school athlete, a standout who held down a full-time job while living on her own and supporting herself.

His work has appeared in *USA Today* and several Midwest sports publications, and he has covered the Kansas City Chiefs, the Kansas City Royals, and the University of Kansas basketball team. Althaus was cohost of the Royals pre and postgame radio broadcasts in the early 1990s and did the last live radio broadcast with Hall of Famer George Brett before Brett retired following the 1993 season. Althaus is a frequent contributor to local and national sports-radio talk shows.

Althaus and his wife Stacy live in Grain Valley, Missouri. They have two sons—Zach, a golfer and business student at Rockhurst University, and Sean, who attends junior college. Priest Holmes, Dante Hall, and Kansas City Chiefs bandleader Tony DiPardo were the subjects of Althaus's previous books.